# ON
# MODERN
# MARRIAGE

*and Other Observations*

# ON
# MODERN
# MARRIAGE

*and*

*Other Observations*

## BY ISAK DINESEN

*Translated by Anne Born*
*Introduction by Else Cederborg*
*Afterword by Frank Egholm Andersen*

ST. MARTIN'S PRESS / *New York*

Design by Manuela Paul

Library of Congress Cataloging-in-Publication Data

Dinesen, Isak, 1885–1962.
    On modern marriage.

    1. Marriage.   2. Love.   I. Title.
HQ734.D624   1986       306.8'1        86-13862
ISBN 0-312-58443-1

First Edition
10 9 8 7 6 5 4 3 2 1

# CONTENTS

# ON
# MODERN
# MARRIAGE

*and Other Observations*

# Introduction: Karen Blixen—
# Her Life and Writings

## BY ELSE CEDERBORG

In "The Cardinal's First Tale" Karen Blixen writes that "a name
is a reality, and a child is made known to himself by his name."
However, in this as in most of her stories the name is of crucial
interest as the signifier of a character's true identity. For instance,
in "The Dreamers," a young man does not seem to attain anything like a personal identity until he is called by the nickname
"Pilot," which "makes him known to himself." He is a mirror
figure for the main character, the opera singer Pellegrina Leoni,
who has lost her voice, her true self, and therefore changes
identities throughout the story. When the young man follows her
example, thereby escaping an empty life, he finds an identity, and
also happiness.

Few writers have been so concerned with the symbolic
impact or sheer suggestive power of the names of their characters
as Karen Blixen. For her the name is very often one of the main
keys to the character, which is made even more interesting by the
fact that she herself carried on a lifelong play with highly symbolic names and pseudonyms. Until the release of the Academy
Award–winning movie *Out of Africa* in 1985, she was known to

the English-speaking world not by her real name, but by her pen name, Isak Dinesen. "Who was this enigmatic Danish woman who changed names the way other people change their clothes?" one asks, when confronted by this multitude of differing names. Obviously, they were important markers in her life and thus keys to her personality and biography, just like the mottoes she used to trace her own development in the essay "On Mottoes of My Life."[1]

Her childhood name, Tanne, probably arose out of her difficulties in pronouncing the "k" in her first name.[2] This name stayed with her all her life, but it was used only by relatives and close friends. Another much more exclusive childhood name was Byron, which she went by with one friend who named herself Arabella.[3] Just as this adaptation of Byron's name signals an identification with rebellion and a voluntary social estrangement, so does her first pseudonym, Osceola. In her biography of Karen Blixen, *Titania,* Parmenia Migel explained that Karen Blixen's father, Wilhelm Dinesen, had a dog named Osceola and that this name had an American Indian origin, but the significance of it escaped her. As Judith Thurman points out in *Isak Dinesen: The Life of a Storyteller,* the original Osceola was the chief of the Seminoles, who fought against the compulsory transfer of his people from their native Florida. He even defeated the American troops in several battles, but was betrayed and died in prison.

Osceola's name is Seminole for "Rising Sun" and has a definite symbolic ring to it, which—along with his being a rebel

---

[1]"On Mottoes of My Life" was first given as a speech in America, January 28, 1959. It has been published in *Daguerreotypes and Other Essays* (1979).

[2]Frans Lasson and Clara Svendsen, eds., p. 32. Many English-speaking friends changed the name to Tania.

[3]The real name of Byron's wife was Anna Isabella Milbanke, so that the pet name should have been Annabella.

of mixed heritage—must have appealed enormously to Karen Blixen. In "The Caryatids, an Unfinished Tale" *(Last Tales)*, [4] an Indian named Osceola is depicted as having the ability to split himself into two personalities, so that "while he was grooming his sleek˙ horses and tying up their tails, [he] was also trotting upon a trail in the woods or sitting in the snow and howling at the terrified mares and foals." In this story the name is given magic qualities. But when Blixen published her first short story, "The Hermits," in 1907, which was followed in 1909 by "The Ploughman" and "The de Cats Family," [5] it might have been enough for her that her father had named his dog after the brave Seminole chief.

When she was born on April 17, 1885, the second of three daughters, later to be followed by two brothers, she entered a family in which there was a dichotomy between the characteristics of her mother (and her relatives) and her father. The people of her mother's family were upright Unitarians, but with very marked bourgeois standards, whereas her father, who was related to Danish and Swedish aristocracy, was an adventurous and unconventional man. As a young man he had fought on the French side in the Franco-Prussian War (1870–71), and for some years he lived with Indians in North America as a trapper. The articles he wrote about this experience [6] reveal that his views on the American Indians as "Noble Savages" would later be reflected in

---

[4]According to a letter by Karen Blixen to her friend Birthe Andrup, this tale about witchcraft, incest, and women's emancipation was her attempt at writing a "modern story," which to her meant "without a definite ending."

[5]These three stories were republished in Danish in *Osceola* (1962), ed. Clara Svendsen (now Selborn). Only "The de Cats Family" has been translated into English. It was published in *Carnival: Entertainments and Posthumous Tales* in 1977.

[6]One of these was published in the Danish magazine *Tilskueren* (1887), in which Karen Blixen made her debut as an author with "The Hermits" (1907), and where she published various pieces later on.

his daughter's views on the natives of Africa (see *Out of Africa* and *Shadows on the Grass*). After marrying Ingeborg Westenholz in 1881, Wilhelm Dinesen became a politician and author. His best-known books are those he wrote on the hunt under the pen name "Boganis," Indian for hazelnut.

According to Karen Blixen, she was her father's favorite child, and he often took her out into the woods to teach her about nature. She felt that she resembled him, and that he alone understood her, whereas she had the feeling of being a foreigner to her mother's family. When her father committed suicide some weeks before her tenth birthday, it was a very traumatic experience for Karen. In a letter to her mother in the autumn of 1921 she wrote:

> I think my greatest misfortune was Father's death. Father understood me as I was, although I was so young, and loved me for myself. It would have been better, too, if I had spent more time with his family; I felt more free and at ease with them. I feel that Mama and Aunt Bess and the whole of your family,—and Uncle Aage when he was out here,— if they care for me at all, do so in a way in spite of my being as I am. They are always trying to change me into something quite different; they do not like the parts of me that I believe to be good.[7]

Objectively, she had good opportunities for exercising her talents as a child and as a young girl. She was allowed to study

---

[7]It is noteworthy that Blixen's child characters, Jens and Alkmene, from "The Dreaming Child" and "Alkmene" *(Winter's Tales)* respectively, both are very artistic orphans who are not understood by their conventional and unimaginative foster parents.

to become a painter, just as her older sister was given all the support she needed when she wanted to train as a singer. The "oppression" she felt was of a spiritual rather than a basic, material nature. A major concern with her very prudish maternal family was morals, which in its turn led to many restrictions and prohibitions on the young, fun-loving, and intellectually alive girl. On the other hand, in her father's family she found much of the physical and psychological freedom she yearned for. Consequently aristocracy came to represent for her the qualities that she would put such store by all her life.

Ingeborg Dinesen and her strong, exceedingly matriarchal mother, Mama, were very close, and naturally became even more so after the death of Wilhelm Dinesen. Since her formidable maternal grandmother, and her spinster aunt, the equally formidable Aunt Bess, a devout Unitarian and a feminist, both took an active part in the upbringing of the Dinesen children, the young Karen Blixen lived her childhood in an overpowering matriarchy. In "Alkmene" *(Winter's Tales)*, she has given her interpretation of the cramping effects of a too moral, too unimaginative upbringing on an artistic child, who is subdued and eventually ruined, not by lack of love in her foster parents, but by too much of it, as these righteous people make it impossible for her to realize her own personality. They rule by love, by being good in the conventional sense of the word, just as the matriarchal triumvirate—Ingeborg Dinesen, Mama, and Aunt Bess—had done in the young Karen's life.

On the other hand, her childhood obviously gave her many opportunities for growth and happiness that other writers have missed. Just as the Brontë children in the beginning of the nineteenth century had been able to create their own fantasy world in the Angria and Gondal juvenilia, so the Dinesen children at the end of the same century could live out their imaginations. Karen Blixen started to write at a very early age; in my critical selection of her juvenilia, *BLIXENIANA 1983,* [8] I have collected and commented on the poems and fairy tales she wrote when she was eight years old. Her brothers and sisters performed her plays with her, and we have a very amusing photograph of the young actors dressed up for *Pride Goeth Before a Fall* [9] by the eleven-year-old Karen, who, for once, has a female part, being dressed in old-fashioned woman's attire. We know from casts in her copy books that she usually took male parts in her own plays, just as all her pen names were masculine, which, of course, is in the tradition of early women writers. [10]

The girls had their own secret language, called "Pirogets." [11] The word in itself means "the language," being a rather lame anagram for the Danish word *sproget,* constructed by inserting an "i" and moving the initial "s" to the end of the word. Judging from its composition, the word might have come from one of those self-invented languages that rely on a very simple construction, but as nothing has been found in writing it is impossible to decide what the grammar and syntax were. However, as the sisters Karen Blixen and Ellen Dahl spoke Pirogets even as old women, perhaps traces of it *may* be found in the more fantastical name constructions of her characters.

On October 13, 1907, she made her debut, not as a painter

---

[8]*BLIXENIANA 1983* contains fragmentary juvenilia by Karen Blixen of which none has been translated.

[9]See Lasson and Svendsen, eds., p. 42. This play has not been retrieved.

[10]Male pseudonyms for women writers were common in Denmark when Blixen published her first stories, but not when she started on her real career as Isak Dinesen in 1934.

[11]Lasson and Svendsen, eds., p. 199. The three girls were close in age, but six to nine years older than the boys, who also were close in age.

but nonetheless as an artist, publishing a cartoon in a humorous paper under the pen name "Peter Lawless."[12] This highly symbolic pseudonym was another of the childhood names that certain good friends knew her by. In the copy books of her juvenile writings, we also find the name "Nozdref's Cook," which she had discovered in Nikolai Gogol's *Dead Souls* (1842). The character from this novel is a man who designs his dishes by inserting "a little of everything," without measuring the ingredients. As there are no recipes, the taste of the food can never be prefigured, the result being a question of the instincts of the cook and the preferences of those who eat his dishes. However, this was not only one of her childhood names but the pseudonym she chose for the collection of short stories, *Nine Tales by Nozdref's Cook,* that was eventually published as *Seven Gothic Tales* in 1934.

The wish for rebellion expressed at all levels in these early pen names actually came to very little. In 1914, when she married the twin brother of the man she had been in love with for years, the action may in many respects be likened to an escape from the "pleasant, loving, infinitely kindly family milieu"[13] that Karen Blixen felt was engulfing her in dull cosiness. As the bride of the Swedish Baron Bror von Blixen-Finecke, she could now join the aristocracy that was forever connected with her father's memory, and her notions of freedom and adventure. This also meant becoming a farmer in Kenya, since the young couple had bought a coffee farm with money from her family, who held shares in it, giving them control. Bror was appointed manager of the farm even though he had an extremely limited knowledge of agriculture. It soon turned out to be a disaster.

---

[12]The cartoon is reprinted in *BLIXENIANA 1982.*
[13]*Letters from Africa 1914–1931,* p. 247: April 1, 1926.

He was also a Don Juan in miniature, taking part in the erotic exploits for which Kenya at this time was absolutely notorious.[14] Unfortunately, he contracted syphilis and subsequently infected his wife, who had to return to Denmark for treatment a little over a year after the wedding. The illness was checked, but the effects stayed with her, and throughout her life her health suffered. In letters to her brother,[15] she claimed that she found her bad financial situation and continuous lack of money much worse than her illness—a claim that can perhaps be explained by her lifelong craving for "style," for "showing off." Even as an old woman she wanted to entertain, to dress well when she had the opportunity to do so, and to live on a grand scale.

Four years after her wedding, Karen Blixen met the dashing English army pilot Denys Finch Hatton, who was the second son of the Earl of Winchelsea. Like Bror, he was a big game hunter[16] and safari leader, but most unlike him he was a very well read man who knew his classics by heart. When they became lovers some years later, Finch Hatton stayed on the farm for weeks at a time, and she told him some of the stories that were later to develop into the tales she published. She saw him as an invaluable critic, but suffered from his lack of personal commitment toward

---

[14]See James Fox, *White Mischief;* Judith Thurman, *Isak Dinesen,* p. 118; and Errol Trzbinski, *Silence Will Speak: A Study of the Life of Denys Finch Hatton and His Relationship with Karen Blixen.*

[15]Thomas Dinesen and Karen Blixen were very close at this time, at least until his marriage in 1926. For the money problems, see the letter to TD of September 5, 1926, and others.

[16]See Trzbinski, *Silence Will Speak,* and Thurman, *Isak Dinesen.* As for Bror von Blixen-Finecke, he seems to have been the original of Ernest Hemingway's great white hunter, Robert Wilson, in "The Short, Happy Life of Francis Macomber." Blixen depicted him as the competitive and shallow Guildenstern in "The Dreamers" from *Seven Gothic Tales,* Denys Finch Hatton being Lincoln Forsner.

her. From the letters it is obvious that she wanted to marry him, and that she might even have tried to lure him into a marriage by pretending to be pregnant.[17]

Strangely enough, she had not wanted to divorce Bror. When he had his way in 1921 and they were separated, it was definitely against Karen's wishes, and she had opposed it in every way. Earlier, her maternal relatives had already urged her to divorce her philandering husband, who had also squandered her money and was a disaster as a farm manager, but she had defended him. After the separation, the letters to her family back in Denmark kept reiterating her regret that the marriage was to end. An extract from one letter to her mother on January 23, 1922, is typical:

> —even though I have occasionally been angry with Bror or, rather, perhaps, in despair over his behavior, there is far, far too much binding us together from all the years and difficulties we have shared here, for me to be able to take the initiative in putting an end to what, if nothing else, was a most intimate companionship.—In many ways my relationship with Bror was a problematic task,—one that I believed to be the most important of my life,—and that I have been quite unable to fulfill.

That she saw her marriage as a "task" is as interesting as it is consistent with the age-old female notion of being the redeemers of men. Still, Blixen did not use the word "task" in that way, as she had no urge to "raise" her husband morally or consciously.

---

[17]While Blixen might have had a miscarriage in 1922 (cf. *Letters from Africa 1914–1931,* p. 137), her second presumed pregnancy (in 1926) has the bearing of a "love test."

Her ambition was at quite another level, but it is impossible to determine which one. A theory, broadcast by her young relative, Anders Westenholz,[18] is that Bror was the man she really loved, being physically very attracted to him, whereas Denys was more of a "Muse" to her. Be that as it may, it is at least safe to say that she did not want the divorce, and that she defended her husband on all occasions against her family. In part this could be explained by their having opposed her relationship with Bror; she had had to force their acceptance of the engagement in 1912. A divorce from him would then mean another defeat by the family she felt had subdued her by always being "right."

The woman who writes *On Modern Marriage and Other Observations* is thus separated, her divorce to be made absolute in 1925. Her health is shattered, and she lives in a trying economic chaos, more or less controlled by the same people she has rebelled against all her life, but who control the shares in the farm she has come to think of as her own. Held captive in this double bind, she also has to come to terms with the fact that her lover does not want the sort of commitment she seems to be yearning for, even though this is not her explicit wish. With this background to the essay, it is strange to see how detached she is, compared to the woman raging at her destiny in some of the letters to her brother.[19]

In the essay, she does not even refer in a direct way to her own experiences; on the contrary, she hides behind a parapet of literary quotations and references. She is trying to surpass the limits of her own personal experience to get to the objective truth

---

[18]Anders Westenholz, *Kraftens horn: Myte of virkelighed i Karen Blixens liv* (1982).

[19]The most famous of these letters is the so-called Lucifer-letter, dated April 1, 1926. Thomas Dinesen has told about their childhood and later relationship in his book *Tanne* (1974), which has not been translated.

about modern marriage and love relationships, but the unevenness of the essay, and the often somewhat forced argument, reveal that she is fighting very hard to make it all fit together. *On Modern Marriage and Other Observations* somehow resembles an adjuration to the pieces of her life's jigsaw puzzle to fall into their proper places.

Blixen seems to take for granted that the feudal form of marriage is the basis of the institution, which of course is historically incorrect. What she likes about it is that it was built on an idea—the inviolability of the family and of the name. By representing their social role, man and woman gained a symbolic worth, thus transcending their individuality. This means that she is focusing on something other than the love relationship which is the axis of the bourgeois ideology: the contract between husband and wife, securing each one's position in relation to his or her spouse and to society at large.

According to Blixen, the type of marriage that came into being with the appearance of the bourgeoisie in the eighteenth century degenerated into a stifling cosiness in the ensuing Victorian era. This kind of middle-class paradise is always the butt of her most intense irony, and it is actually her prime dislike, but she does not take too kindly to the institution of marriage in the twentieth century either. In this case her complaint is not with the hypocrisy or the suffocating cosiness of the nineteenth century, but with the lack of purpose and meaning. By turning into a kind of "free love," modern marriage rests, in her opinion, on shaky ground. It does not mean anything in itself, thus being nothing but a "figleaf" because of its lack of ideals. People do not know how to handle the new situation, and with love as the only lodestar they often get lost.

When in Chapter XI ("Intermezzo") she insists on the

necessity of women also learning to play, Blixen seems to be foreshadowing the so-called New French Feminists, who see *jouissance* (sexual rapture or pleasure) as a liberating force.[20] She is fully aware that women have had to pay a heavier price for their participation in the sexual game, and therefore recognizes what birth control means in their lives. Actually, she seems to be dividing female history into a pre- versus a post-birth-control era, making the ability to avoid pregnancies the turning point.

With eugenics as her bid at a new "Heavy Child" for humanity to carry, so that it can once more lead a life full of ideals and honor, she has come to her own kind of turning point. Apparently this idea engrossed her fully for a year or so in Kenya when she was reading such writers as George Bernard Shaw, H. G. Wells, and Samuel Butler, but later on she seems to have given it up altogether. Apart from *On Modern Marriage and Other Observations* and a few references to the topic in her letters, it left no perceptible traces on her writings.

Over the years Karen Blixen had spent long periods in Denmark, either to be treated for her illness or to see her family. The letters to Thomas reveal that she often wanted to give up her struggle with the unyielding soil, but the alternative of returning home a complete failure and having to live with her mother put her off. In the end she had to give in, as the farm was sold in 1931 by the family company, Karen Coffee Co., at a forced sale. Only three months before she went back to Denmark, Denys Finch Hatton was killed in an airplane crash. However, it seems that their relationship had already ended by that time.[21]

---

[20]Cf. *New French Feminisms: An Anthology,* edited by Elaine Marks and Isabelle de Courtivron, especially the Introduction.

[21]See Thurman, pp. 246ff.

One of her regrets at leaving was her concern for her African servants, who had played a great part in her life in Kenya. In *Out of Africa* and *Shadows on the Grass* she has given a vivid portrait of several of them, immortalizing the Somali Farah and the Kikuyu Kamante. Reading *Letters from Africa 1914–1931,* one realizes how she has made them into larger-than-life characters. Yet by gaining these almost mythical proportions, they have not lost their intrinsic humanity. Just the contrary, one might say, knowing well that most of the characters in her fiction are also endowed with the same larger-than-life qualities.

After the sale of the farm, Karen Blixen, now forty-six years old and totally destitute, had to take up residence with her mother. This dreaded solution to her plight of course had many drawbacks, just as she had foreseen, but on the whole they got on very well. Economically supported by her brother for the first two years, Karen stayed with her mother until the latter's death in 1939. Then she lived on at the family residence, Rungstedlund, where she had been born, and where she was eventually to die herself at the ripe old age of seventy-seven.

It might be said that Karen Blixen's life falls into three main stages, indicated by the changes in her names and thus her identity. As a child, she had been Tanne; then she became the baroness von Blixen-Finecke, and that title she kept even though Bror made two more women baronesses by marrying them. She enjoyed being addressed as "Baroness," although this was frowned upon in democratic Denmark. But perhaps after all she liked her third name and identity the best: Isak Dinesen.

This new pseudonym, which came into being when she published *Seven Gothic Tales* in 1934, took its symbolic impact from two sources. The first name, Isak, refers to the biblical legend of the old and hitherto barren Sara, who laughs when she hears that she is going to give birth to a boy. When she then does conceive, she calls her son Isaac—"the one who laughs." To Sara it had been a divine joke, a postmenopausal miracle, and so it was to Karen Blixen, who came home as the prodigal daughter, broke, ill, and disillusioned, but who all the same could "give birth" to a book and a new identity. Probably it also meant something to her that Isaac was saved by God when his father thought he had to sacrifice him.

That she kept her family name may had have another reason, aside from the most obvious one. "Dines," etymologically derived from "Dionysos," might have appealed to her because of its Nietzschean implications. Both the philosopher Friedrich Nietzsche and the Greek god of wine and free-flowing inspiration always had a strong appeal to her.

In 1944 she used another pseudonym, Pierre Andrezel, when she published her only novel, *The Angelic Avengers,* but this time she did not want to own up to it. The book was for fun and nothing more, she claimed, and her anonymity thus ought to be respected. Even though the novel may be just "for fun," it is not without interest, since it deals expertly with white slavery and the dualism in a Christian, patriarchal society.

Up to her death on September 7, 1962, she enjoyed entertaining, being with people and going places. Among her close friends were several young poets or otherwise artistic men. With one in particular, Thorkild Bjørnvig (born 1918), she had a relationship that might be called a "spiritual love affair."[22] An-

---

[22]Blixen gave her version of their friendship in "Echoes" from *Last Tales.* Here she once more donned her alter ego from "The Dreamers" *(Seven Gothic Tales)*, the opera singer Pelegrina Leoni, who has lost her voice—i.e., her identity. She strikes up a friendship with a young man to bring out his potential as a singer. In his book *The Pact: My Friendship with Isak Dinesen,* Thorkild Bjørnvig describes their very close relationship. According to him, she seems to have had an almost devastating impact on his private life because of her possessiveness.

other extremely important person in her life was her secretary for eighteen years, Clara Selborn (then Svendsen), who was appointed the literary executor in her will, and who thus has kept on working for the promotion of the books even after Blixen's death.[23]

Throughout Blixen's works we find an overt aim for unity, expressed at all levels. This goes for *On Modern Marriage and Other Observations* as well, and, since it is an early piece, it is obvious that this was a longstanding, crucial matter with her. Her main complaint in this essay is that what is wrong with so many people, love relationships, and social institutions in modern times is that they do not bring about any real unity. For her, this "Unity" always consists of disparate elements fused into an entity by some superior, mutually shared idea, as stated in "Farah" from *Shadows on the Grass:*

> In order to form and make up a Unity, in particular a creative Unity, the individual components must needs be of different nature, they should even be in a sense contrasts. Two homogeneous units will never be capable of forming a whole, or their whole at its best will remain barren. Man and woman become one, a physically and spiritually creative Unity, by virtue of their dissimilarity. A hook and an eye are a Unity, a fastening; but with two hooks you can do nothing. A right-hand glove with its contrast the left-hand glove makes up a whole, a pair of gloves; but two

---

[23]Clara Selborn (née Svendsen), born in 1916, has published several articles on her employer and friend. In her biography *Notater om Karen Blixen,* which has not been translated, she tells of the eighteen years she worked for Blixen, of their travels together (for instance to the USA in 1959), and of the people who came to see the famous author.

right-hand gloves you throw away. A number of perfectly similar objects do not make up a whole—a couple of cigarettes may quite well be three or nine. A quartet is a Unity because it is made up of dissimilar instruments. An orchestra is a Unity, and may be perfect as such, but twenty double-basses striking up the same tune are Chaos.[24]

Even though not all the examples of unities given here are that exalted, it is evident that the passage concerns something of vital interest. Great things are at stake if the alternative to unity, as defined by Blixen, is chaos. The fear that the relationship between man and woman will eventually decline into a chaotic medley of forces, pulling in opposite directions instead of working together as a unity, is not only at the core of the early essay *On Modern Marriage and Other Observations* but of all her works. In "Farah" she says that "a community of but one sex would be a blind world." If this "blindness" can be seen as the punishment awaiting the modern man and woman for letting go of some of their traditional sex role characteristics, then the reward for keeping up this game will be the "inspiration" she talks about in another essay, "Oration at a Bonfire, Fourteen Years Late" (1953):

I myself look upon *inspiration* as the greatest human blessing. And inspiration always requires two elements. I think that the mutual inspiration of man and woman has been the most powerful force in the history of the race, and above all has created what is characteristic of our aristocracy:

[24]Isak Dinesen, *Out of Africa and Shadows on the Grass* (New York: Vintage Books, Random House, 1985), p. 408. One of the most potent unities to Blixen is the one between master and servant. She felt that she and Farah formed such a unity.

courageous exploits, poetry, the arts, and the refinement of taste. I think that one of the ways in which human beings have elevated themselves above animals is this: human beings mate the year round—a society in which the attraction of the two sexes to one another was limited to a distinct, brief period, must become notably blunted. Yes, I think that the more strongly the mutual inspiration functions, the richer and more animated a society will develop.[25]

Simone de Beauvoir, in her treatise *The Second Sex,* claims that it is a very unhappy thing that woman throughout history has been cast in the role of "the other," the sex who is always an object even to herself, never a full subject.[26] In complete contrast to de Beauvoir, whose opinion was adopted by the modern feminists in the 1970s and 1980s, Blixen saw "otherness" as a necessary part of one's identity, whether man or woman. Interestingly enough, we can trace the development of her feminism in *Letters from Africa 1914–1931* by focusing on two subjects. One is the Somali women; and the other is the expression "the love of the parallels," which she borrows from Aldous Huxley.[27]

In the early 1920s, Blixen is full of hope for women and their future. She exhibits a true feministic anger at the subjection of the female sex, and she thinks so much about the whole matter of the relationship between modern man and woman that she writes a lengthy treatise on the subject, *On Modern Marriage and*

---

[25]Isak Dinesen, *Daguerreotypes and Other Essays* (London: William Heinemann, 1979), p. 70.

[26]Simone de Beauvoir, *The Second Sex,* translated and edited by H. M. Parshley (New York: Alfred A. Knopf, 1953; first published in 1949). De Beauvoir's theory is explained very well in her Introduction.

[27]Aldous Huxley, *Crome Yellow* (1921) and *Those Barren Leaves* (1925).

*Other Observations.* Then, around 1928, she begins to have misgivings about the situation in modern society, which does not
allow women the position of honor they held in former times.
On January 13, 1928, she writes her sister, Ellen Dahl:

> I think that there has been another great change, that per-
> haps people are still not conscious of, in that the idea, so
> to speak, has disappeared from womanliness, of what it is
> to be a woman. I think that the women of the old days,
> and especially the best of them, felt themselves to be repre-
> sentatives of something great and sacred, by virtue of which
> they possessed importance outside themselves and could feel
> great pride and dignity, and toward which they had a
> weighty responsibility. Neither the arrogance of the young
> and beautiful girl nor the majesty of the old lady was, after
> all, felt on their own behalf; they were without any element
> of personal vanity, but were borne as something to take
> pride in, a shield or a banner. Where a personal affront
> might well be pardoned, a violation of that womanliness
> whose representatives they were could never be forgiven;
> a blow might perhaps be overlooked, but never a stolen
> kiss. I think very few young women in our time feel any
> of this.

Like so many other women writers,[28] she starts out on a
social crusade under the banner of "changes and emancipation,"
only to end up by regretting the mystery and the interpersonal
power women have lost by gaining equality. In several letters she
makes horrified comments on the lives of the Somali women,
whom she sees as extremely suppressed. However, around 1928

---

[28]Cf. Figes, Fleenor, Moers, Spacks, Showalter, and others.

she begins to talks of the special dignity which she thinks that the absolute seclusion from "the men's world" gives them.[29] In *Out of Africa,* and in Danish interviews from the same time, she expresses the belief that they really obtain power and dignity from living in a totally sex-divided society. What is most interesting is that she draws a close parallel to women's situation two or three generations back from her own. Since the bulk of her tales were set in the historic time of the rising bourgeoisie, her portrayal of the Somali women in *Out of Africa* gives us a key as to her views on women's tactics and self-understanding during the Victorian era.

In a letter to Thomas Dinesen of August 5, 1926, Blixen uses the phrase "the love of the parallels" to give her vision of modern man and woman living in a new kind of unison, which she has earlier characterized as a positive form of spiritual "homosexuality"[30]:

> Aldous Huxley has an expression: *"The love of the parallels,"* which he uses in a somewhat tragic context, it is true, but which I must surely be permitted to construe as I like, —which to a certain extent expresses what I mean by this: one does not "become part of," become "devoted to," the other; perhaps one is not as close to the other as in those partnerships that are able to encompass such merging, and there is no question of each being the aim and goal of the other's life, but while one is oneself and striving for one's

[29]The Somali women are discussed in, for instance, the letters of January 8 and 13, 1928; June 24, 1928; March 17, 1929; and April 13, 1930.

[30]In a letter to Mary Bess Westenholz, May 23, 1926: "I think it is possible to think that such a 'homosexuality'—sincere friendship, understanding, delight shared by two equal, 'parallel moving' beings—has been a human ideal that conditions have prevented being realized until now."

own distant aim one finds joy in the knowledge of being on parallel courses for all eternity.[31]

Yet in what is considered her most reactionary writing, the ultimate proof that she was not a feminist—the essay "Oration at a Bonfire, Fourteen Years Late" (1953)—she has come to the exactly opposite conclusion: "In one of his novels about a sterile and painful relationship, Aldous Huxley uses the expression, 'the love of the parallels'—that hopeless love between two parallel lines which stretch out simultaneously but can never meet."[32] The problem is that men and women get too close to appreciate each other, like a priest and his wife who remain together in the same house all day, thus missing out on the magic and the mystery of sexual attraction.[33] The ideal relationship develops only where there are distance and dissimilarity between man and woman, as is the case with, first and foremost, the sailor and his bride. While the woman, being a woman, is supposed to be repelled by the feminine symbol of the sea, the man proves his masculinity by being attracted to it.[34] Blixen's ideal man is the sailor, who has not lost himself in intellectual speculations like so many of her male characters, who become what she calls "dreamers." In "The Dreamers" *(Seven Gothic Tales),* a definition is given by one of the characters, the "much renowned story-teller Mira Jama":

"You know, Tembu," said Mira suddenly, after a pause, "that if, in planting a coffee tree, you bend the taproot, that

[31]*Letters from Africa 1914–1931,* p. 264.

[32]Isak Dinesen, "Oration at a Bonfire, Fourteen Years Late," from *Daguerreotypes and Other Essays.* Translated by P. M. Mitchell and W. D. Paden. (Chicago: University of Chicago Press, 1979).

[33]"Alkmene" and "Peter and Rosa" from *Winter's Tales* deal with this conflict.

[34]The elements are used as male and female symbols in the traditional manner. Very often this is the key to the story.

tree will start, after a little time, to put out a multitude of small delicate roots near the surface. That tree will never thrive, nor bear fruit, but it will flower more richly than the others. Those fine roots are the dreams of the tree. As it puts them out, it need no longer think of its bent taproot. It keeps alive by them—a little, not very long. Or you can say that it dies by them, if you like. For, really, dreaming is the well-mannered people's way of committing suicide."[35]

Like Plato,[36] Blixen believed that man knew what he was, from inside, so to speak. This means that man can realize his potential by acting out his innermost feelings, wishes, and desires, which are seen as closely linked with biological and psychological needs. Another way of saying this is that man is a "marionette," or rather, that he ought to allow himself to be directed by his God-given instincts like a "sacred puppet."[37] This is what the ideal man in Blixen's works, Simon from "The Sailor Boy's Tale" *(Winter's Tales)*, does, and it brings him happiness as he realizes his potential as a man. Unfortunately, most men cannot do this, as they will not let themselves be guided by their instincts, or perhaps have even lost them altogether. Instead of *being* what they *are* and living accordingly, they use their intellect to figure out what to do, which means that they very often go wrong. In "The Heroine" *(Winter's Tales)*, a young woman makes a reference to the seventeenth-century Dutch philosopher Spinoza.

---

[35]Isak Dinesen, *Seven Gothic Tales* (Frogmore, St. Albans, Herts: Triad/Panther Books, 1979), p. 234.

[36]Ca. 428–348 B.C. For an explication of this idea, cf. the *Republic*.

[37]This expression is used by the dying Councillor in "The Poet" from *Seven Gothic Tales*. The marionette theme itself plays a crucial part in *The Revenge of Truth*, which is a very early play, and in "The Roads Round Pisa" from *Seven Gothic Tales*.

Why she does so is clear from the story: she ought to have been loved by the young man, but he was too much of an intellectual to understand intuitively what to do. Like Spinoza, Blixen in her appreciation of the instinctual places intuition higher than rationalism.[38]

The fact that most human beings do not know how to live by their instincts, thereby doing "the right thing," is tied up with Blixen's views on the Fall. She seems to think that when man gained his soul, he lost the close instinctual contact with God. However, those who do understand how to live end up like the man in "The Roads of Life" *(Out of Africa)* by "seeing the stork." This expression stands for a special kind of understanding of one's fate, as "the stork" is the pattern made up of one's life. But such felicity occurs only when a person fulfills his or her destiny by following the course he or she feels is right in spite of all kinds of hardships.

Like Plato, Karen Blixen thus believed that man was born with an understanding of "God's intention with him." Ever since the first drafts of *The Revenge of Truth* (ca. 1904), she had touched upon this concept in her writings. In "Of Pride" *(Out of Africa),* she elaborates on it:

Pride is faith in the idea that God had, when he made us. A proud man is conscious of the idea, and aspires to realize it. He does not strive towards a happiness, or comfort, which may be irrelevant to God's idea of him. His success is the idea of God, successfully carried through, and he is in love with his destiny. As the good citizen finds his happiness in the fulfilment of his duty to the community,

---

[38]Spinoza's theories on the three kinds of knowledge are elaborated in the *Tractatus de Intellectus Emendatione* and in the *Ethics,* part II.

so does the proud man find his happiness in the fulfilment
of his fate.[39]

Whereas men are attracted to the female symbol of the sea,
women very often want to fly up into the sky, and they are
frequently described in bird images. However, this is not without
its problematic effects on the relationship between men and
women. In "Daguerreotypes" (1951), Blixen tells about a woman
—she is a witch—who has this strong urge to fly, who "existed
independently of a man and had her own center of gravity."[40]
Other women are supposed to have their center of gravity in
man, but the witch is the liberated woman who follows her own
course. "Supper at Elsinore" from *Seven Gothic Tales* contains a
discussion on women that is very illuminating. One of the female
characters, who has many witchlike attributes, has just said that
she would fly if she had wings, which is a rather alarming
statement to the Bishop:

> "Indeed," he went on, warming to his subject, his glass still
> in his hand, "in woman, the particularly heavenly and
> angelic attributes, and those which we must look up to and
> worship, all go to weigh her down and keep her on the
> ground. The long tresses, the veils of pudicity, the trailing
> graments, even the adorable womanly forms in themselves,
> the swelling bosom and hip, are as little as possible in
> conformity with the idea of flying. We, all of us, willingly
> grant her the title of angel, and the white wings, and lift

---

[39]Part IV of *Out of Africa*, "From an Immigrant's Notebook," consists of thirty-two short philosophical prose pieces, "Of Pride" being one of them. The quotation is from Dinesen, *Out of Africa and Shadows on the Grass*, p. 271.

[40]The concept of a "center of gravity" relates to the marionette imagery, as puppets cannot move without it.

her up on our highest pedestal, on the one inevitable condition that she must not dream of, must even have been brought up in absolute ignorance of, the possibility of flight."

"Ah la la," said Fanny, "we are aware of that, Bishop, and so it is the woman whom you gentlemen do not love or worship, who possesses neither the long lock nor the swelling bosom, and who has to truss up her skirts to sweep the floor, who chuckles at the sight of the emblem of her very thraldom, and anoints her broomstick upon the eve of Walpurgis."[41]

The woman who is not allowed to have her center of gravity in a man because she is rejected by him, in her frustration may become a witch. Old women, like Miss Malin in "The Deluge at Norderney" *(Seven Gothic Tales)*, are supposed to get their center of gravity back into themselves after menopause, which, if nothing else, makes them witchlike. Amiane in *The Revenge of Truth* (1926) and Sunniva in "The Sailor Boy's Tale" are old witches with magic powers, which they use to bring about the right conditions for others. These old fairy tale–like witches are not emancipated in the ordinary sense of the word. Actually, only two female characters in the works of Karen Blixen become witches by choice, both of them being young and beautiful. They are Simkie and Childerique in "The Caryatids, an Unfinished Tale" *(Last Tales)*, in which it is said that "it was as if he, the house and garden of Champsmelé and all the life awaiting her there were pale and cold in comparison with the world of witchcraft."[42]

---

[41]Dinesen, *Seven Gothic Tales,* p. 203.

[42]Isak Dinesen, *Last Tales* (London: University of Chicago Press Ltd., 1957), p. 150.

Another way of having one's center of gravity in oneself is simply by being too young to know about love. The adolescent girl has a certain lightness in body and soul that almost sets her flying. Robin Lydenberg comments: "A magical weightlessness and an imminent possibility of flight emblemize for Dinesen this tenuous adolescent freedom she prizes so highly. Shifts in an individual's consciousness are often measured in *Seven Gothic Tales* in relation to the law of gravity."[43] This, however, goes for other stories as well, even though it is true that it is closer to the surface in her first work than in her later published books. People of strong feelings, but with a certain kind of innocence, often have a "balloon"-like quality, as she calls it. This goes for Prince Potenziani of "The Roads Round Pisa" as well as for Fransine from "The Poet" (both in *Seven Gothic Tales*), even though they seem extremely different. What they have in common is their innocence, which allows the Prince to play God and Fransine to edit reality to meet her own dreams about it. In Fransine's case, it leads to tragedy: she loses her lover and, like so many other female characters in by Blixen's works, thereby suffers a loss that can be discerned in her very body as she ends up looking like a "stick"—without her female form and characteristics.

Woman's means of survival in a man's world lies, according to Blixen, in duplicity, double-talk, and mystery.[44] Her own example of a woman who masters this world without losing one inch of her femininity is Portia in Shakespeare's *The Merchant of Venice*. In the essay "Oration at a Bonfire, Fourteen Years Late," she writes: "Her magic lies precisely in her duplicity, the pre-

---

[43]Robin Lydenberg, "Against the Law of Gravity," p. 528.

[44]A depiction of this system at work may be found in "The Somali Women" from Part III of *Out of Africa*. For the phenomenon of women's "double-talk," cf. Elaine Showalter, ed., 1985, pp. 243ff.

tended deep respect for the paragraphs of the law which overlies her kind heart and her quite fearless heresy."[45] In this essay, which might be seen as Blixen's "last will" concerning feminism and the relationship between men and women, she gives voice to the opinion that now that woman has won her case, she *is* man's equal, and does not have to fight for her rights anymore. Whereas her fiction is radiant with indignation at women's conditions in a double-standard society, her essays seem detached and even a little tired of the whole thing. Only occasionally, in short paragraphs, does she show any strong feelings. This detachment does not, however, save the essays from being rather uneven.

When "Oration at a Bonfire, Fourteen Years Late" was published in 1953, it gave rise to a long row of indignant protests from feminists. What they were so upset about was the statement that "a man's center of gravity, the substance of his being, consists in what he has executed and performed in life; the woman's, in what she is." So, whereas men have "to do," women have "to be," according to the sixty-eight-year-old Karen Blixen, who in the 1920s had rejoiced at all the things women now were able to do—and who certainly had been a "doer" herself, both in Kenya and after. Somehow her own achievements do not seem to have counted with her; and as to her being a successful author, in the same essay she denounces female artists who try to do more than reproduce men's ideas or music. This means that a female author is unfeminine, whereas an actress does not lose her femininity. To watch this change in views is sad, even though it is obvious that to her, "being" is so much more than "doing," just as it was for Aristotle and Thomas Aquinas. The same kind of development seems to be consistent with a number of women

---

[45]Dinesen, *Daguerreotypes and Other Essays*, p. 83.

writers, so many of whom have started out as feminists, fighting for social changes, only to end up adhering to female mysticism.[46] In her African letters, Blixen had protested against women being held captive on pedestals; but later in life she wanted them honored through a new elevation of the so-called feminine qualities.

The nineteenth-century Danish philosopher Søren Kierkegaard was of the opinion that there are three stages of human development, the religious, the ethical, and the aesthetic, of which the first is the ultimate goal one can strive for.[47] With Karen Blixen it is almost the other way around, since she denounces the ethical as cramping and even ruinous—as it had been to her in her childhood—and the religious and the aesthetic seem to be the same. Seeing instinct and a life according to nature as the highest goal, the aesthetic, of course, is her choice of an ideal lifestyle. In Kierkegaard, the aesthete is Don Juan; in Blixen's work, this person may be the sailor or the artist, even though they are extremely different. What they have in common is their close connection with God, as both of them lead a life that seems ordained, whether through instincts or divine inspiration.

Another character who shares these qualities is the aristocrat, who is seen as being on the same level of development as the wild animal—and one cannot do better, in Blixen's opinion. In "Farah" *(Shadows on the Grass),* she makes a definite distinction between wild animals and domestic animals.

One of the reasons for idealizing the aristocrat is Blixen's own adherence to the radical existentialism she found in the works of, among others, Friedrich Nietzsche and the nineteenth-

---

[46]See, e.g., Figes, Fleenor, Moers, Spacks, Showalter, and others.
[47]See Kierkegaard's *Either-Or* (1843).

century Danish critic and writer Georg Brandes. The latter, who was considered extremely radical and even immoral at the time, was one of the heroes of her youth, representing a spiritual and physical freedom she yearned for.[48] Both Nietzsche and Brandes were believers in the form of inner nobility that she saw in the aristocracy. Usually she employs an aristocrat to carry these characteristics, but they are not in fact socially determined. In *Out of Africa,* for instance, she uses the concept to explain the differences between the native races and tribes. The Masai, who have never been slaves because they die in captivity, are seen as the aristocracy of the natives: "This stark inability to keep alive under the yoke has given the Masai, alone amongst all the Native tribes, rank with the immigrant aristocracy."[49] It is not, then, a matter of being born into a noble family, but of having a special attitude toward life.

Many of her short stories turn upon the clash between aristocratic and middle-class ideologies. However, this is her way of saying something about psychological and ideological matters, and it is more of a metaphor than a political statement. On various occasions[50] Blixen said that only by setting her tales back in time could she become free. In the same manner she seems to have created a host of characters who attain archetypal status by infusing them with special, definite characteristics that go with their type but at the same time may be something quite different. This is all very contrived and not at all in accordance

---

[48]See Thurman, pp. 60ff. Georg Brandes introduced Nietzsche in Denmark in 1888. He was interested in the German philosopher because of their shared belief in the noble individual, the "Superman" who transcends the limits of his time and society. Brandes was also known by the name "Lucifer."

[49]Dinesen, *Out of Africa and Shadows on the Grass,* p. 156.

[50]For instance in interviews in Denmark, one being that in *Politiken,* May 1, 1934.

with her repeated insistence that she was an exponent of the oral tradition:

> I belong to an ancient, idle, wild and useless tribe, perhaps I am even one of the last members of it, who for many thousands of years, in all countries and parts of the world, has, now and again, stayed for a time among the hard-working honest people in real life, and sometimes has thus been fortunate enough to create another sort of reality for them, which in some way or another, has satisfied them. I am a storyteller.[51]

Her choice of the Gothic as her genre goes very well with this contrivance. According to modern scholars, it was a genre that was adopted by women writers dealing with oppression and victimization as the best vehicle for expressing rebellion or a muffled protest.[52] Obviously, the Gothic genre furnishes the author with the same freedom as, say, science fiction writers find, because both are limitless in their fantasy elements. The rules are made up by each individual author; thus Blixen can employ at her convenience a device such as that of a prioress turning into a monkey in "The Monkey" *(Seven Gothic Tales)*. She was very attracted to the theater of the absurd, but she would also have been able to appreciate good science fiction writers as kindred spirits.

Because Karen Blixen's works are so contrived, it is obvious

---

[51]Quoted in Donald Hannah, *"Isak Dinesen" and Karen Blixen: The Mask and the Reality*, p. 60. For a full discussion of the impact of the oral tradition on Karen Blixen's writings, cf. Merry Weed (1978).

[52]See, e.g., Eva Figes, *Sex & Subterfuge,* Chapter 5: "The Gothic Alternative"; Ellen Moers, *Literary Women,* Chapter 5: "Female Gothic"; and others.

that the message is part of her aesthetics, and vice versa. As Sibyl James has indicated:

> Given Dinesen's attitude toward the imagination, it is not surprising to find that she replaces the Gothic emphasis on moral sentiment with an emphasis on the imagination which works for her as a kind of moral sentiment. She also replaces the direct authorial preachiness, the self-important solemnity that we find, for example, in [Ann] Radcliffe's passages on St. Aubert's efforts to train Emily in the proper brand and degree of sensibility. Instead, Dinesen makes a more indirect presentation of her message through in-set tales; through a more symbolic use of events; and, in most typically Dinesenian fashion, through witty conversation. This last method relates to her speaking of the Gothic she drew on as imitation or artificial Gothic. The very modernness of her treatment lies to a great extent in just this awareness of the artificiality of the Gothic trappings, in a self-consciousness that is part of the wit yet does not mock or parody the Gothic.[53]

It is very easy to misread Blixen because she employed a special genre, which she nevertheless expanded to meet her needs, and because she furnished literary characters like the aristocrat with qualities that were easily mistaken for something quite different. What, at least in Denmark, was seen at first as aberrant snobbery was eventually understood as the claim for life fulfillment, for honesty, and for human dignity. It has been the same with her feminism, and Sara Stambaugh is right when she points out that "because her stories are difficult and because she claimed

---

[53]In Julian E. Fleenor, ed., *The Female Gothic*, pp. 140ff.

not to be a feminist, the intense feminism in the stories of Karen Blixen, known in English as Isak Dinesen, is only beginning to be noticed."[54]

*On Modern Marriage and Other Observations* may surprise those who took at face value Karen Blixen's statement, in "Oration at a Bonfire, Fourteen Years Late," that she had never been interested in feminism. Now that we have more keys with which to open up the secrets of her writings, we can see that it was crucial to her throughout her life.

---

[54]Sara Stambaugh, "Imagery of Entrapment in the Fiction of Isak Dinesen," p. 171.

# On Modern Marriage
# and Other Observations

## BY ISAK DINESEN

### Translated by Anne Born

## *I. On the Ideal and Nature*

I was still young when I left Darwin's desert and entered the
verdant gardens of Lamarck.

What fruits the trees bore here! All of those that human
beings have seen in their most felicitous dreams: beauty, knowledge, eternal youth—indeed, everything you could wish for.

Can you visualize any new perfection at all, are you able
to formulate a new desideratum and really imagine something
truly desirable—then look up! It is already hanging on the green
branches.

The fact that it is hanging rather high up is merely a joke,
a kindly leg-pull, just as when a mother hangs a sweetmeat so
high up on the Christmas tree that her little child has to stretch
his utmost to get hold of it.

So far nothing has been out of reach. The only question to be asked is: What would you like?

The rule is always the same: What you wish for, you shall have.

Art creates a new, strange, preternatural type, extracts it from the unconscious longings of men, and the next generation is born with this appearance. For there is no essential difference between the ideal and nature, but a difference of degree.

It is a question of time as to when the ideal changes its name and calls itself nature.

We wished to get rid of our tail—if we wish to get it back again doggedly enough we shall wake up one morning and find it there.

Do some of you want to fly? Is it something you really want, and does the idea attract you more than anything else? Then hang on to your wish for a couple of thousand years and you will get wings.

Many generations have said of whatever they considered most impossible: "It's as impossible as flying." Indeed, people are still saying it, but they are flying. If there is anything to be learned from this it is that nothing is more impossible than flying.

Now people say: "It is as impossible as flying to the moon." But we cannot fly to the moon because we do not want to do it, at least we nourish no burning desire to do it. The inhabitants of earth are not so strictly denied knowledge of the secrets of the universe; they are unknown because man has as yet no great wish to know them.

It is the same as with the secrets beyond the grave, very few really wish to know about them.

Then do not many of the conflicts of humanity arise out of the desire for too many things and out of wishes that are at variance with each other?

The giraffes conceived a desire to eat the new shoots on the treetops and stretched their necks up toward them for many thousands of years until their desire was completely fulfilled. But with that, the ambition of the giraffes seemed to have been satisfied, and the next millennia brought about no significant change in their nature.

Complex human beings have many desires, and change their tastes from generation to generation. May they not risk breaking their necks or getting their heads turned through such disparate strivings?

Although it needs a wiser person to answer this, it can at least be said that frequently things appear to be so without really being so, for as small children we drink milk for the same reason and with the same result with which we later eat roast chicken, and dress in wool in the winter and in muslin in the summer to keep at the same temperature.

The pendulum does not turn round and change direction because its direction is found to be the wrong one, but the clock works because the pendulum moves to and fro.

Art develops through wild romanticism, onward through fiercely pragmatic naturalism. It has not changed course in its striving, it has always sought to be the expression of human longing. A person taking a Turkish bath does not change his opinions because he first makes use of water that is as hot as he can possibly tolerate and ends up with the coldest; nor would he achieve the same effect of well-being and invigoration if on entering the baths he had immediately filled a common pool with water of every degree of heat.

Then again the same things viewed in different lights can look quite different.

In certain Somali tribes no young man can marry before he has killed a man. This does not necessarily mean that these tribes are especially bloodthirsty; it may just as well signify that conditions among them are so warlike that a young man who has not by the age of twenty taken part at least once in a struggle for life or death is most probably a coward, whose offspring would be undesirable for the tribe.

A similar development is reflected in the European ideal of virginal innocence, which has gone out of fashion owing to changed conditions.

In former times when women from the upper classes were surrounded by multiple moral walls, it was felt that a girl who could envisage the opportunity of involving herself in a love affair, indeed, even concerning herself with love at all, must be "full of the devilment," and any sensible man might well have misgivings about marrying her. In the twentieth century it is equally taken for granted that a girl who in the modern atmosphere of freedom and eroticism gets to the age of twenty-five without once at least having believed herself to be in love would generally be thought either unusually dead or unusually calculating, and must give to her intended reasons for doubts of a different kind.

Sometimes, too, individual words may, owing to circumstances, change their meaning . . . as when it was an English soldier's greatest source of pride to have been one of the "Contemptibles."

## II. On Doubt and Struggle

In the whole history of man no ideal has been relinquished because it involved too many difficulties, but old ideals were rejected because they had lost their sheen and no one wanted to adopt them anymore, or felt really attracted by them.

In the long run there is no effort, danger or suffering that can stop humanity striving to achieve an ideal, but the ideal's hour has come when people in general begin to question: "What good does it do?"

Nowadays when people do not allow themselves to be burned or expelled from society for the sake of Paradise, it is not because our more refined nerves cause us to fear the stake or poverty or expulsion more than our forebears did, nor because we are in doubt that our sufferings will gain us entrance to Paradise—for in any case such a belief could easily spring up at any time at all—but because the Paradise that is promised us in connection with these sufferings does not appeal to us. We have no desire for it and would have no wish to go there even if access to it were free.

On the other hand, when people began to believe fervently that bliss was to be found in motorcars, a good cellar, and so on, then the majority were prepared to undergo frightful sufferings for years, in offices, factories and stock exchanges, in the hope of finally attaining that bliss. At this moment probably fifty percent of civilized humanity would be reconciled to enduring all the pangs of the early Christians if they knew they would emerge on the other side with an annual income of £50,000 [$200,000 in 1923] for the rest of their lives, and so for them there is no reason to envy the victims of Nero—with eternal bliss in store for them—their strength of character.

Many women undergo sufferings that amount to daily flaying in order to preserve, not their youth but an appearance of it, and would go through anything at all to recapture the real youth that for them represented Paradise.

It is perpetually the idea of paradise that is the dependent factor, and if a sufficiently attractive illusion can be created, the reality automatically follows. This is true for every undertaking —as with the building of St. Peter's—in that it only begins to make headway when in some way or other it becomes concerned with salvation.

(Now St. Peter's does stand there, and we who doubt whether the souls who contributed to it in their time were thereby saved must yet rejoice that the whole enterprise was embarked upon.)

It is therefore incorrect to say, for instance in connection with love's role in life, that this ideal or that is too high, even though it might in itself be desirable. It has always been clear that no ideal was too high. At the beginning of the nineteenth century, when the ideals that brought salvation were those of romanticism, it was the easiest thing in the world for young lovers to wait for the whole of their lives, to die of sorrow, to build their lives on the memory of a youthful attachment, to burst into tears, to swoon on reunion.

To the young people of our day who do not want all this, who ask what good it does, it would seem difficult if not impossible. But the things that the young people of today find easy to do would have appeared no less difficult to Werther and Lotte —for instance, to break up, quite calmly, a relationship that has lasted for years, or a marriage and a family without further fuss because of an argument.

When Nora resolved to embark on this because it was a case of salvation for her, the general opinion was that it was all treated much too casually, and that the whole problem was almost impossible to solve; but now it happens every day and is not regarded by anyone as a special tour de force.

Do you want to be Sigurd and Brynhild, Romeo and Juliet? —If you really want it, you will get it.

Do you want to be Klister and Malle, are you deep down more attracted by this?—Then it is what you are already.

Is your real ideal to be a tomboy? Well, you have been so for a long time.

An ideal like faithfulness in marriage or complete chastity has shown itself perfectly possible to carry through in the era when it led to a paradise of some kind or other, and would be possible to carry through today if people did not ask: "What good does it do?"

Poets of later times who have dwelt on the sufferings of young monks for the sake of the ideal of complete chastity are interpreting their own feelings when they make the young monk think he would rather be a bandit in the mountains with his sweetheart than a friar in the monastery, or they are thinking of a time when the sheen had disappeared from this ideal. For the first Franciscans, whose hearts were burning with faith, with love for the Holy Virgin and with longing for Paradise, it was no harder to live in poverty and chastity than it is for Carpentier to keep himself in condition during his training for a match with Dempsey. Future times, when boxing has gone out of vogue, will arouse sympathy for the sufferings of boxers in the twentieth century in verse and prose in the same way.

It is said that in matters of love or faith, personal will falls short, but the truth is that nowhere does it reveal itself more strongly.

I will take an example in the matter of faith from Martensen-Larsen's book *Doubt and Faith.* It describes the attempt of a modern human being with a very strong desire and will to believe to reconcile the belief in the Atonement through Christ's death with modern science and morals.

For the detached reader this is really an exciting struggle, for the task seems impossible from the outset, and yet it is clear that the person writing has staked all his peace of mind on conquering. It is like watching someone trying to "loop the loop," and, if you have not seen it done before, thinking it is impossible . . . the only reason for hope is the burning desire, the will to succeed of the person making the attempt.

And look! Through this, and only this, it really does succeed. We read how the author continues to persevere in spite of the fact that one attempt after another ends in failure. Finally a verse from the New Testament, a word of Christ's—which obviously could have been any word at all that he hit upon—produced the wonderful effect: the attempt has succeeded, he believes.

The author sees this so clearly that although he does not give himself all the credit, yet finally, while contemplating his success, he turns to those weaker spirits whom he had urged to follow suit but whose courage failed them, and reproaches them, saying that they could certainly believe if they really wanted to, but that their will is weak. He is perfectly in the right here, and the doubters are only evading the issue when they say that they *cannot* believe this or that. What they really ought to say is that they have no desire at all to believe it, and the believers would find this much more convincing.

If doubters felt really attracted by the idea of the Atonement and Christ's Resurrection, or by the thought of a just Providence to whom they could pray in case of need, it would be perfectly easy for them to believe—indeed, many of those who declare themselves unable to believe have given proof of quite a different capacity in the direction of believing, and build their lives on talking to their dear departed through a table. But these ideas do not attract them; they have no desire whatsoever to believe in them.

Certain peripheral difficulties arise in spite of everything in periods of transition, when human beings are confused about their ideals or the means of effecting them, so that for instance they think they can win a boxing match by the sort of preparations that can lead them only to Paradise.

## III. Modern Marriage, or "What You Will"

It often happens that what survives longest of a venerable institution is its name, because for many people the word holds more reality than the idea.

Sometimes all parties concerned may be satisfied with a state of affairs where the contents have wasted away while the shell is intact, and the suggestion that the name should be abolished would be greeted with outrage at a time when the idea and the thing itself had crumbled away like dust in the grave.

As a rule, the empty shell can remain standing as long as there are children of the real believers living, the kind of people who take their concepts from parents in whose time the contents really were present.

Even perhaps as long as there are children alive of those

again, who can recall the piety of their parents when the word was mentioned. This, for example, is the case with the idea of Christmas, or the Christmas spirit, for the words, the melodies, the scent are still hallowed through the memory of the voices of those people for whom the sacredness of it was reality, and this is confused with the thing itself. The illusion may be extended so far, that, for instance, even rice porridge and doughnuts, which are not normally highly regarded, acquire eminence on this occasion as festive fare, with an air of sanctity.

So it is with modern monarchy, for example, which has preserved its name and something of the luster appertaining to that of the old kind—although neither Harald the Fair nor Louis XIV would have given any acknowledgment to or, without explanation, have recognized the present institution at all as being the royal one.

There are probably still many people today who feel their hearts beat faster when they receive an honor from the king's hand, and they are not aware that their hearts are actually beating at the echo of their faithful grandfather's voice when he took them to watch the changing of the guard at Amalienborg Palace. But they are not afraid in these same hearts to call the king a sh-- when he behaves in a different way to that which they consider fitting.

It is often the case with a new idea that when it comes knocking at society's door with modesty and the best premises for its existence, there is a tremendous outcry from inside.

All are agreed that if this idea ever penetrates society, the state of things will be doomed.

The entire civic guard is called out to barricade the gates and the clergy is usually ready to invoke protection against the enemy from the pulpit. When a certain amount of security has been achieved in this way, the excitement recedes and little more is heard for a time about the idea, and the next thing one either hears or sees of it is that it is sitting on the Lord Mayor's right-hand side at Constitution Day dinner.

Nobody knows how it has got in, and this is therefore a question left in abeyance.

I will take ladies' corsetless dresses as an example.

I have lived through a time when this question really made the headlines. The newspapers—not only ladies' journals—published articles about it, and the corsetless outfit was called reform dress. But the corsets carried off the victory that time. True enough, there were those who agreed that corsets could be somewhat shorter and looser, but it was impossible for a lady to have a well-dressed appearance without corsets, for how could a dress be made, and how could it fit properly without them? No one was able to answer this question, and corsets grew longer and longer.

After the matter was thus settled, little more was heard about it. And now, fifteen years later, you can walk through all the fashionable salons, theaters and restaurants and not see any corsets at all. The young women who create the fashions and will have nothing to do with reform dress would not dream of ruining their silhouettes with corsets. The problem of how to make and fit dresses has been solved, although no one can really explain what actually brought this about.

If at this moment a suggestion should be put forward whose aim was quite simply to abolish marriage, it would probably even this very day meet with a great deal of resistance. Perhaps it would be regarded as revolutionary in some quarters.

Why? Because many of the old partisans of marriage are still alive, those who carried its flag in the fight against free love many years ago and conquered.

You old partisans of marriage! Did you never in the heat of battle look hard enough at the face of "free love" to be able to recognize it when you meet it again?

Open your eyes. It is free love that has its place in the heart of the bourgeoisie. The clergy bless it. The Lord Mayor keeps a record of it, it wears a ring, it has annexed the scepter and the orb of marriage, the esteem of society and the very name of marriage.

## IV. Modern Marriage, or "What You Will" (Continued)

The confusion of marriage with morality has done more to destroy the conscience of the human race than any other single error.

—Bernard Shaw

If there should be an attempt—for instance by a vote among modern educated people—to get an answer to the question: "What is it that changes a relationship between a man and a woman from an immoral to a moral relationship?", then in ninety-nine out of one hundred cases the answer would be: "Love."

This shows that modern educated people have a fairly correct and true idea of what morality is, and what love is.

But if the same group should be asked: "What changes a

relationship between a man and a woman from a free relationship to a marriage?"—that is to say, morally and ideally, for I am aware of the legal aspect, at least just at this moment—then most modern educated people would be quite at a loss to find an answer. For modern educated people have no idea what marriage is.

It would be interesting for once to look at the possible answers that might be given.

For instance, would any modern human being dare to oppose the law and the spirit of the law so much that he would answer: "Its indissolubility"? At most he could perhaps suggest: "Its longevity," and there might then be established a time limit for when a free relationship changed into a marriage.

Or would he dare to oppose the spirit and morals of the time to such an extent that he would emphasize the worthiness of the desire to increase and multiply mankind and maintain that this is the essential difference between the free relationship and marriage?—with the risk thereby of transferring half the total number of worthy marriages into the free relationship category.

Might it be thought that the answer would be: "Its lack of concealment, its acknowledgment by the State," as a (dubious) moral justification on the part of those who have most eagerly opposed the frankness of free relationships—indeed, consider them to be the more shameless the more frankly they are acknowledged—and who certainly would not make any attempt to raise the standing of those relationships of another kind that are provided with the blessing of state recognition, or at least were until a few years ago.

Perhaps the answer would be: "Faithfulness, or fidelity." At least this would be one answer to be desired, for nothing reveals more clearly than the interpretation of the concept of fidelity how far people today have lost sight of the idea of marriage, while they have the whole of the moral and ideal code of free love at their fingertips.

For according to the moral law of free love, infidelity is a deadly sin as long as the relationship lasts.

Where love is the highest, indeed, the only law, a defection from it is an annulment of the whole relationship. In the relationship of love, infidelity equals that sin in the relationship with God that is called "against the Holy Ghost." And in the same way, where infidelity is concerned there can be no difference of degree, but the least and the most bear the same mark of perdition.

But in marriage? Should not frailty here, in an aspect that is not a matter of salutation, be forgiven for the sake of the higher ideals?

Of course marriage has been obliged to take account of so many other sins, and not only within its own four walls, for it had a position in regard to the world outside, and sins against the world outside rebounded onto the marriage itself. A spouse who diminished his esteem or ruined his good name sinned against his marriage, and his partner could demand reparation, while a lover could do nothing about it.

Should there not be tolerance on this point?

And must not the modern view of life willingly admit that when it has itself worked to get the law to dissolve a marriage for a single lapse from fidelity, it has by this acknowledged marriage to be a love relationship?

## V. Modern Marriage, or "What You Will" (Continued)

It is easy nowadays to visualize a young man of undisputed honesty, well versed in today's code of honor, who on a journey, at a seaside resort, or at "<u>winter sports</u>"\* meets and falls in love with a girl so deeply that he is convinced that his greatest happiness would lie in winning her, and only later gets to know that she is married.

Now there have been times when the honorable young man would have had to regard the affair as closed, even if it seemed to both parties that they were having to renounce all the joy and harmony in life.

Or in other times when for a young man holding the highest concepts of honor it must have seemed different—that the barriers dividing them had been placed there by both heavenly and earthly powers. Their love would have to be as secret as the stars of the night, or else everything—position, family and friends—would have to be sacrificed for it, and their bliss built on these ruins.

Nowadays things are different. This marriage is an obstruction against which he has every right to pit all his energies. It may take some time, but this gives the lovers an opportunity to show the strength of their feelings and win the sympathy of those around them.

They have the law on their side as well as the prophets.

In this situation a marriage is in a less favorable position

---

\*Words underlined denote that Karen Blixen used English in her original text.

than a free relationship in the same circumstances. A modern, honorable and idealistic young man acknowledges love, and holds its eternal rights in veneration; he may perhaps have scruples about breaking into a love relationship that do not apply at all to marriage.

And the same is true in the matter of sympathy from those about them. For when marriage threw away its old weapons in order to show itself off in the beautiful garments of love, it exposed itself to the danger of having these weapons turned against it. Now when it is attacked, it has only the rights of love to invoke, and it would be a mistake to bring out the old considerations of family, property, or position, for they only arouse suspicions about the pure unmixed love under whose flag it is sailing. Perhaps he married her for money and so deserves nothing else than to lose her?

Then let us—to furnish more proof of how marriage has also assumed the second great commandment in the code of free love: "<u>Unhesitating, uncomplaining acceptance of a notice of change of feeling from either side</u>"—give some consideration to the third person in the comedy, the husband or wife, and see how they stand morally and ideally in modern marriage.

Since the modern husband is an honorable young man with a highly developed code of honor, in this conflict he can only win or lose, in an honorable and decent manner, under the sign of love.

If as a lover he can win back the wife he was about to lose, it is an honorable victory, he has humiliated his fellow wooer and can celebrate a triumph . . . even novels and plays have treated this aspect.

If he cannot win back her love, but she loves the other man more than she loves him, he must submit to the rights of love, and can gain a certain amount of sympathy thereby, even though he is standing in the shade when the radiance of triumphant love is shining on the happy pair.

But if out of self-interest he demeans her and himself by persuading her to continue in their life together without love, he will find that one and all are against him, for there is nothing more despicable in the whole bible of free love than a lover who tries to force love by outward circumstances, with old dead promises, with material values. To the modern view of life this is a struggle between the spirit and the letter, already lost in advance.

Then with what weapons should a marriage carry on the struggle?

In the old days, spouses who were threatened fought for an idea when they fought for marriage—or they could at least take an idea with them when they went into action that would be in their own interest. As a last resort they could fall back on the Church, or God Himself.

Now that fifty percent of marriages are performed in a registry office, there is no longer any reason to believe that God takes any special interest in them . . . on the contrary it is probably the general opinion that he is on the side of love.

They used to make use of home and children as their most powerful argument, but these too have lost weight, for what good can it be to a home or a family that those who direct it have betrayed their highest ideal? It is surely much more likely to have the effect of a kind of curse, just as it was when a crusader would adopt Islam for any reason whatever; just as when, in days of yore, honorable young wives for the sake of their child, indeed, to save its life, submitted to those in power and sold their "honor."

The importunate spouse can only wage a purely formal battle for his or her name or position in society, for what meaning does a name have in modern society, and what can actually be said against the position of divorced wife or husband, which a large proportion of the nation probably accepts without a qualm?

What remains are purely material considerations, for which no one can have sympathy in a matter where love is concerned; and it is surely better for the rejected spouse to accept the situation with resignation as soon as possible, or to take a piece of good advice: to try his luck in a new love . . . go and do thou likewise!

I ask you, could this have happened among honorable people with a true sense of honesty, for whom marriage had a reality, an idea? And the capacity of the word to survive the thing can once again be seen here, from the fact that for many people there still exists an idea that marriage is more moral than a free relationship.

## VI. Modern Marriage, or "What You Will" (Concluded)

If this judgment should be correct, and there should be discussion of moral values, then modern marriage is at most the wolf in sheep's clothing, and even then the wool is pretty thin.

This really means nothing more than that society has come to a tacit agreement with itself that if only it is tarred in a certain manner with ink from the registry office, a sheep can really perfectly well have this appearance, and howl like this.

But this is not actually so. A better metaphor might be to say that just as out here [i.e., in Africa], for instance, we inoculate cattle against certain diseases, after which we brand them with a certain mark to show this has been done, so it was in former times with marriage. It was assumed that a certain idea had been implanted into the mental life and way of thinking of the couple, and the Church and the law set their seal on this to be shown to the surrounding world.

But a considerable percentage of those inoculated die during the process, and society might have many other reasons as well as this for concluding that it was not worth undertaking. If nevertheless it still seemed to preserve the branding and a certain reverence for it, it would have to be assumed that this was because of one of two views: either that the brand in itself possessed miraculous powers that extended to the whole process—which could hardly be thought to survive as a conviction among modern educated people—or that the brand looked well from the purely aesthetic point of view, and contributed to a civilized and complete appearance. The moral aspect of the whole affair was not worth mentioning, of course. So it is with modern marriage.

Perhaps there still exists, among those who a generation ago took part in the battle for marriage against free love—and won —the idea that marriage is in general rejected for aesthetic considerations but is preserved for moral reasons . . . but in fact the reverse is in reality far more likely.

Even these old champions of marriage, who think they are on secure moral ground, must, if they would for once ransack their own hearts and brains, admit that they are confusing the eternal rights that work for the benefit of humanity with their own personal taste—a confusion that is still to be found even in the most honorable people, but nowhere more often or more fatefully than in everything to do with love—and with pious zeal have been fighting for considerations of beauty and decency when they thought they were striking a blow for such high ideals, which are a sine qua non for humanity.

There is no accounting for tastes . . . one must be excused for quoting this old maxim as long as there seems to be a need to have it confirmed, for nothing is more vehemently disputed. Whether one is carried away by an ordinary young, bashful housewife, or a beautiful, congenial lady friend, or a Valkyrie and guardian angel, must be a personal matter, and is only of interest insofar as the personality is interesting. There is no doubt that hearts can beat and be inspired at the thought of her who "is to step into the lady's bower, and purity and peace shall hold her company," just as much as for her who is "awesome like the sight of a banner . . . and the charm of her glance, that is a bugler who carries us away," or for that dream that can never be attained and possessed, whose "soul became a song in your breast—myself will you never capture" . . . and poetic dispositions can be equally moved by each of them. On the whole it is probably true to say that free love in poetry and art has been rather more honest than marriage, which was quite prepared to play a few tricks in this direction, where ideals of beauty and what was "respectable" were concerned. But then it did occupy an easier position; and on the whole, of course, there is no reason for not raising your hat when time is up for a line of thought or a trend in ideas that has brought much beauty to the world.

A certain era existed (and is still alive in our own time) which was reluctant to—there has for some generations been a shrinking from—look love, as a natural force or divinity, in the eyes.

Whereas the young generation of today would run to greet

Venus Anadyomene rising from the sea with delight and palm branches, the representatives of this age, who still hold the responsibility for our mores, would turn away or hide their faces. This has been interpreted as contempt, but in fact it is the attitude adopted by that high-minded generation toward what for them represented the highest in life, and which certainly looks back on a very estimable tradition—as when Mohammedan law requires the young free woman, the most valuable of life's goods, according to its view of life, to be draped from the knees to the neck and calls her body "shameful," while a female slave can wear much lighter clothing without offending against the law.

Here one can discuss higher or lower sensitivity of interpretation, and perhaps both sides may talk of tastefulness or tastelessness—but there is no accounting for tastes.

This generation, which has arranged our marriage customs and occupies the place of honor at our weddings, is averse to, if not finding it quite impossible to have any part in, the establishment of a love affair. And so the lovers, out of consideration for this attitude, hide themselves with a greater or lesser degree of coquettishness behind family and position, house and home. Upon marrying, the bride changes her name from Miss Rosenfeldt to Mrs. Løvenskjold; this can be talked and joked about, and one is not concerned about what else may be happening.

Modern marriage has thus become a figleaf, which can certainly be discussed from the aesthetic point of view but which morally must be said to be valueless.

The opponents of this concept of beauty and modesty have nothing to say against it other than that it is not theirs, and that for this reason they renounce it and all its being. The younger generation, who have a taste for, who see ideal beauty in nakedness—from dancers with bare feet to the so-called naked truth in all relationships—openly enter into their marriages as love affairs and celebrate their weddings as festivals of love. And when after all it is in love with, and still retains, the traditions, these imperceptibly change significance under a new illumination of life, so that the bridal veil which is kept and treasured symbolizes already less those unacquainted with love than those initiated into love.

It is of no use for the older generation to maintain that their taste in these matters was better, for there is no accounting for tastes, and of modesty it may be said that it is satisfied when established custom has received its due . . . or could it be imagined that this older generation would dispute that to the pure, all things are pure?

## VII. The Great Emperor Otto

The great Emperor Otto
Could never decide on a motto.
He hovered between:
"L'État c'est moi" and "Ich dien."

When Kormak was wooing Stengerde and thinking of their future joy, he sang to her:

"In passion's flight
we are moving nowhere.
Under Freja's arches
joyfully we rest.

> All the music of rejoicing
> hastens toward us."

But it happened that

> "the girl replied
> and gave me answer:
> 'Flying in passion's flight
> we go toward our goal.
> Through Freja's arches
> joyfully we'll glide,
> for our happiness beckons
> on the other side.' "

Then he preached to her of free love, but she answered him with marriage, and from these differences in understanding of the love relationship, and the happiness it brings, came all their misfortunes.

For where love is the highest law, and Freja's arches the ultimate goal, there the relationship between man and woman is a love relationship, and when regarded ideally, a free love relationship, even though they are married by headmen and priests, as Kormak and Stengerde agreed to be.

But the love relationship between a man and a woman becomes a marriage when it is entered into in the recognition that the personal feelings of both partners—no matter how much they had based upon them—must be subordinate to, and serve, an idea that for both of them is higher than love itself, the kind of idea that as a rule exacts the lifetime of both, and whose demands may reach even further.

In the course of time many marriages and free love relationships, like that of Kormak and Stengerde, have foundered on a vacillation back and forth between these two ideals.

After having for a time tried to create love out of marriage, and taken it for granted that it was an easy thing to build love on the foundations of a good and solid marriage, that it would grow up, so to speak, of its own accord, as an adornment of the marriage, this style of building was relinquished. It was found to contain a false calculation somewhere or other, and the whole structure was reversed. So then love was established as the foundation and it was considered that where a strong feeling was the basis, it was easy to build a good and solid marriage.

Society still frequently stops its ears with this theory while the crash of collapsing marriages echoes through our generation.

But a building such as this can at best turn out like the Leaning Tower of Pisa, and seldom has much likelihood of standing so long. For in a free relationship the beloved is everything, the beginning and the end, as Stengerde was for Kormak, but in marriage two personalities meet in an idea, and neither one of them is the most important thing in life to the other, but marriage itself is so to them both. This is the situation between a general and an army, where the most fervent devotion can be seen on both sides: yet the general does not mean everything to the army, nor the army to the general, but the war they are waging is everything to both sides. So it is between a king and a people: the king is not everything to the people, nor the people to the king, but the idea of the kingdom is everything to them both. So it is with a priest and his congregation: they love each other, but the priest is not everything to the congregation, nor the congregation to the priest, but God is all to them both.

So most modern marriages, viewed as marriages and not as love relationships, are like an army and a general staff in a land where war is forever out of the question, a king and a people without a country, a congregation and a priest without faith.

It is obvious to everyone who is in any way concerned about the development and future of humanity and who cherishes the hope that in this respect too it may be able to achieve more beauty, harmony and happiness, that in everything concerning love there is a need for far more clarity, honesty, idealism, than the world has hitherto wished to apply to the subject, and that in our century we are embarking upon a conscious program of education in all matters relating to love, which have been completely neglected.

So if humanity should have a desire to, feel attracted by, and set up as its highest goal an ideal free love, it will be obliged to create as high an idea of love in itself as is possible.

For thousands of years love was preached against as something that was base in itself, and its standing still suffers from this. For many hundreds of years poetry and fiction have expressed the view that the service of love was the easiest of all, and that those who do serve it suffer and are in error thereby.

For in order to live in a free love relationship, the individual has need of high idealism, instinctive recognition of the rights of the individual, and a great sense of beauty . . . since when all is said and done the free love relationship rests on beauty, and the beautiful free love relationship has always represented the highest revelation of this that it is possible to attain.

And it represents more: the capacity really to love, without the support of habit or outward conditions, and to see the highest revelation of the divine—as others see it in religion, the beauties of nature, art, duty, a fatherland—in a single human being, and his own sanctity and salvation in being united with that person.

There is a discrepancy in the view of life at the present time in that theoretically love represents the highest thing of all to most people, yet at the same time they do not seem to feel that it is in this very sphere that they must give the utmost of which their nature is capable. The philosophy of marriage is largely to blame here, but it is at the same time excused because it did not put love as the highest or the holiest. And even though it has been formally rejected, in reality marriage still has so much power over people's minds that most of them limp on both legs in their love affairs—"but so evenly that you can't see it."

Until love is openly acknowledged as an ideal, and ideality is openly demanded in love, most people will receive their education in love—at the same time that they get their education in science, politics, agriculture and art from the best representatives available—from the more unworthy of the servants of love's temple, and as a result will settle down later in life making far lesser demands on themselves for unselfishness, honesty, sensitivity, understanding, and self-control in the service of love than in any other sphere. It is sadly true that if most of the older people alive today were to look back over their lives, they would have to acknowledge that their most contemptible behavior as human beings had been in connection with love.

Yet the most beautiful voices of humanity have sung of love as the highest thing that human life has to offer . . . and in the course of a few thousand years they have perhaps not only made themselves heard as beautiful music, but have penetrated human consciousness.

If humanity should have a desire to, feel most attracted to, and set as its highest goal the relationship of free love, in time all truth-loving and gifted people would see in their love affairs the touchstone of their being.

But if humanity should decide to see something more attractive in, and have more desire for, marriage, then, now, and in the future, it would have need of the idea on which marriage can be built.

For marriage will not collapse because free love, like a will-o'-the-wisp, has lured our time onto marshy ground by showing it an ideal that was pleasanter and easier for many to follow, as marriage itself likes to describe. But it will collapse because of its own terrible lack of idealism, its own willing slavery to the letter, so that a marriage was a marriage, and the most frightful things could be perpetrated within its four walls that for the sake of its good name could not be given the opportunity of being protested against. It will not collapse because its laws are strict and demand sacrifice; nobody would fear this. But it will collapse because it has no heaven beckoning at the end of the road, and because it has no ideal, because the general attitude toward it now is: "What good does it do?" It must therefore prevail on itself to answer this question, or else be relegated in human consciousness to dignified and venerable moribundity in the same way that the holy army and the sacred monarchy have resigned themselves.

If, that is, people do not feel that there are still a few centuries of life left in the basis of simple and plain orthodoxy: that marriage is holy.

The one salvation-bringing Church has been alive for a long time; the one salvation-bringing matrimony may perhaps stay alive for a while still, and there is always a good deal to be said, in the battle between orthodoxy and free thought, for orthodoxy. One immerses oneself in the history of the salvation-bringing Church with increasing wonder at its ability to make human beings sacrifice their own and others' dearest wishes and vital necessities merely by its assurance that they will thereby receive salvation. In the end one asks: "And were they saved?" . . . and is answered: "No, probably they were not saved, but through these enormous sacrifices they did manage to be more satisfied than you seem to be."

If orthodoxy cannot always boast of having achieved peace, it can at least say that if human beings had listened to it and acted upon what they heard, they would have found peace.

There is only one thing that orthodoxy cannot do: it cannot assume the name of ideal.

And human beings desire the ideal.


## VIII. Christopher the Holy

> Reprobus, later known as Christophorus the Holy, was a Syrian chief of unusual girth and strength, who went in search of one stronger than himself, whom he might serve.
>
> —Jacobus de Voragine, *The Golden Legend*


Now the slogan "Art for art's sake" is so familiar that we probably have no real understanding of what it meant when it was a war cry.

If we were hearing it for the first time and without prior assumptions, it is probable that we would understand it as a demand on art, of the strictest kind: "Be art. No pandering to sensation, no borrowed plumes, no bargains with the help of outside effects. Be pure, be art."

But this is not how it was understood; on the contrary, it came from art's own camp, where one would not think that anyone could have found anything to object to in it. On many occasions it seems to have been used as a kind of excuse for the weaknesses of art, and then generally for such works as would now be most severely judged according to the rule L'art pour l'art. Strangely enough, it occurred at the same time that art was claiming the dubious right to extend its domain and to occupy itself with solving moral problems and shifting moral boundaries.

Now most people would agree that this is a very justifiable demand and that those who dispute it take an incorrect view, or a short-sighted interpretation, of the range of art.

To examine this more closely we may take an example from cookery, an art that has a deep-rooted and intimate relationship to life.

It is often said that "the proof of the pudding is in the eating," and this probably refers most often to what has preceded the serving of the dish, being an injunction to the cook not to be too particular about his preparations but to concentrate on making the dish enjoyable, and in particular not to be bound by prejudice. If he can produce a delicious dish out of a handful of dead rats, from the point of view of culinary art he is justified, and in future, rats must be included in the cookbooks as perfectly good ingredients in a meal. But thus understood, this shows a misunderstanding of the range of cookery, for matters do not end with the meal itself, and if the company dies, or even feels very unwell afterwards, the proof of the pudding turns out rather differently.

For instance, one could say that the Borgias' chef was not permitted to practice the principle of l'art pour l'art because in their kitchen the art of cooking was subordinate to political and religious considerations. But here cookery had entered upon a course that in the long run, if it had continued, would have led to its ruin. Mohammedans and Jews must still pay attention to religious considerations in slaughtering and preparing meat, but as far as the Mohammedans are concerned, they have no very high standard of cookery to maintain. Presumably, on such occasions, where art has any say in this connection, at dinners for the great pashas and barons, religious considerations must be waived. And would anyone at all who had a genuine interest in and enthusiasm for the art of cookery, and who was not restricted by reasons of health and finance, engage a cook who did not subscribe to the axiom of l'art pour l'art?

It is not suggested here that even the most passionate cook would not have at least a faint idea that there might be higher purposes in life than cookery. He might even be expected to realize, and not to object to the fact, that his art contributed directly to serve political ambitions, but he would be right to consider that it served these best where it was in itself most excellent as art. In themselves these are in fact a matter of indifference to the ideal art of cooking; it does not prepare a poorer dinner for one political school than for another.

St. Christopher took a different view of life: he wanted to serve, and it was reasonable for him to ask that the master he was going to serve should in some way or other be stronger than he was himself.

So now let the love that is not self-sufficient but wishes to bear "I serve" on its shield, that is to say, let those who still uphold and preach marriage, follow his example, and without shunning any effort—perhaps also like St. Christopher himself possibly without much hope—set out on their wanderings to search for something stronger than itself, stronger than love, and ideally, like St. Christopher, persevere in not wanting to serve, not letting love serve anything that fails to measure up to this demand.

It is liable to be in for a long journey, and in this connection it would be worthwhile for it to take his story to heart, if it could thereby take a shortcut and begin where he ended; that is, for those who know the legend, by serving God. Is there any sense in bringing up this case here and, as it frankly acknowledges that it is not sufficient to itself but seeks something higher and stronger, in asking: "Then is it God whom I must serve?"

Many will hasten to answer yes here. Church, tradition, reply first. But they do not know who they are talking to, and therefore the answer does not hold any reality whatever. The love that seeks, the modern St. Christopher, may take the oath of allegiance with the greatest solemnity, but it will only discover later that it is a mere formula; it takes on no real service, for none such exists.

The fact that modern human beings do not believe in God is of no importance here. No, that is not the point.

For several thousand years the more civilized portion of humanity has proudly claimed to believe in only one god. This monotheism resembles modern marriage, which also calls itself monogamy, that is, it has only believed in one god at a time. The God of Moses would not only not acknowledge the God of Christian Science as being identical with himself, he would be extremely hostile to him. Indeed, it is questionable whether he would not actually believe that it was his old opponent, the Devil, in a new disguise. God's voice in human hearts may possibly sound with the same power and resonance, but its reper-

toire changes completely from century to century, for the God
you are seeking is your own god—what more do you want?—
and the longing for the ideal creates the thought of God. But the
thought of God cannot possibly create any other ideal than the
one that is there already.

The God of the old patriarchs was the God of the tribe, and
therefore God's voice in their hearts spoke on behalf of the tribe,
and thus took the side of marriage.

The God of bygone Germany was the God of the fatherland
and the dynasty, and His voice spoke in favor of marriage in their
interest. The God of old times was in every way the God of the
family, law and order, and thereby of marriage.

But the god of the moderns is the god of the individual,
he is the god of emotion, and one of his first commandments is
that the letter killeth but the spirit giveth life; then one should
surely at least also assume: renders legitimate. An arrangement for
the sake of appearances where the spirit is wanting, a life together
without love, is an abomination to him, his voice would con-
demn it in the heart of every modern young man or woman
. . . and it is even open to doubt whether any clergyman would
be able to prevail upon himself to uphold it in the name of law
or order or any other ideal from the pulpit. He too has taken the
part of love against marriage.

If modern human beings set their ideals in, for instance,
family, fatherland, clan, then they would at once have a god to
impress these ideals upon them and maintain them, and then love
could serve him. But then it would not need him.

So the modern St. Christopher leaves the altar where he had
first knelt and takes up his pilgrim's staff.

## IX. . . . *Sets Out on His Wanderings*

In the course of its development, humanity imperceptibly discards a great many ideals as not merely objectionable but inapplicable.

A discussion arose during a party regarding how many of the ten commandments could be said to be necessary for the highest ideal of modern times—the perfect <u>gentleman</u>—to keep.

Although there was a certain amount of discussion, on the whole opinions were fairly uniform and would probably be much the same wherever this problem came to be debated.

The commandment that the perfect <u>gentleman</u> could not evade was the eighth. Also, the general opinion was that violation of the ninth and tenth commandments should not be a characteristic of the perfect <u>gentleman</u>, although a single case of this probably would not do him much harm. Where the seventh commandment was concerned, everything depended on circumstances. The view was that there are presumably many professional thieves in the world who can be called true <u>gentlemen</u>, and the present day has after all created a kind of ideal in the <u>gentleman</u>-thief Raffles.

As it is generally taken for granted that the perfect <u>gentleman</u> is in a position to be able to ignore the difference between the sabbath and the days of the week, a scrupulous observation of the third commandment might perhaps cast a shadow of doubt over his perfection; but still in itself this cannot be said to have anything to do with the understanding of the perfect <u>gentleman</u>.

But the ten commandments were once given in thunder and lightning from Sinai, and we have no justification for believing any of them to have been incised on the tablets of stone just as padding. On the contrary, we must assume that to take the Lord's name in vain must lower a man's esteem among the moral elite of his time, at least as much as, for example, to have enlarged upon one's conquests in love would have done fifty years ago, or lack of generosity toward subordinates, or the attempt to force or persuade a wife to intercourse that was distasteful to her, or the suspicion of cheating at cards would do today.

This thought of how moral evaluations are thus radically transformed must prepare us to expect that in the future the moral code of our day will seem utterly incomprehensible.

Is it then true that the great concept of the family—which for so many centuries held its place as one of the highest and most incontestable ideals, and for which so much blood, so much strength, so many personal feelings and sufferings have been sacrificed—has now been struck out of the human dictionary? And is it the idea of the family that has taken marriage with it into the grave?

If St. Christopher came to me personally and questioned me on these observations, I would answer yes.

Marriage is built on the family, the clan, the nation, and when the course of development, when the spirit of modern times did what they could to abolish these concepts and all their works and being, and in time tricked them out of what they had appropriated of esteem and property right down to the ground under their feet, they tore away the very foundation of marriage. Then it could not be long before it fell, and its fall was great.

There is no longer any really active material left alive by which to examine the concept of the family. No one can expect that by dealing with it, they will find material that will have a direct influence on or aid for the present time. The whole enterprise would be more like visiting a museum, where it is true that we can sometimes hope that by immersing ourself in the essence of former times we can find something that will assist the understanding of or can indirectly be used in the present.

Let us then, in order to see to what extent a noble family connection realized the demands made on marriage, stop by . . . a tomb. By the tomb of the duchesse de Rohan, who, when she was expecting a child, demanded higher marks of honor because she was pregnant with a Rohan.

Now it must be thought that the concept of Rohan became rooted in the consciousness—in the consciousness of the whole nation as well as in that of the two young people who entered into a marriage for the sake of this family. It represents here certain definite qualities: courage, loyalty to the crown, liberality, chivalrousness; and perhaps, too, some that are not usually regarded as meritorious: hardness, indulgence, or red hair and small eyes. Yet this is of no account. The family is a concept that as such has a part in the history of the country; a Rohan is more (or less) than a human being: he is a Rohan.

Nor is there any doubt in his own soul that it is this quality that is the highest and most significant in his personality; indeed, his whole personality serves it, and gains stature thereby. Whatever personal advantages he may have—good looks, talents, valor —are of value because they can be of use to or cast luster on the Rohan family. The Rohan who believes that through his personal beauty, talents, valor he is something different or more than a Rohan has degenerated from the idea of his family.

Therefore the young duc de Rohan who is about to wed may have met and loved many women from every nation, faith and cast of mind . . . yet there always remains not only a difference of degree but a deeply essential difference between these relationships and their role in his life, and his relationship to a wife. For he has loved, conquered, suffered as a young, handsome, talented, valorous, passionate man, but he becomes a married man in the attribute of a Rohan, the highest idea his life can realize.

The contract that is entered into through his marriage is not a personal concern; what is essential here is that "the woman (and man) of noble birth marries as the man of noble birth fights, on political and family grounds, not on personal ones."

His bride's personality will be judged in the same way as his own, according to its value to the family. Her beauty, wit and efficiency are of importance: it is she who is to wear the Rohan jewels, to do the honors in their house, to keep up the family name in difficult times. Provided that she is useful to the Rohan family or sheds luster on it, she can be casual about the yardstick by which the rest of the world judges her. The young mademoiselle de Rohan who became the wife of the duc de Guise's son, the duc de Chevreuse, was renowned for her adventures and intrigues, but her gifts and charm were still pearls that were quite satisfactory enough to be added to the thread on which hung the rest of the family's precious collection. Brought up and singled out for the service of an idea, she was an acquisition of tremendously great value for the Rohan family; at her wedding she kneeled to receive a task and a name that rested on her brow like a diadem.

The relationship between the spouses was no personal one, and strictly speaking they could not personally or directly bring happiness to or disappoint each other, but must mutually provide the greatest significance to each other through the relationship they occupied and the importance they had for their mutual task in life. For the duc de Rohan, there could never be any real comparison between his wife and other women: no matter how much more beautiful and gifted and attractive they might be, she still remained the only woman in the world who could give birth to a duc de Rohan. The receptions she held were receptions for the Rohans, the poor she supported were the Rohans' peasants and poor.

Even the style of their personal feelings had to be judged in the light of the same idea, so that an intense devotion was of great value to the family and safeguarded its happiness, while a violent personal passion might put it in danger . . . even their intimate life together was carried out, so to speak, in the service of an idea.

On principle, both spouses were probably obliged to close their eyes aimiably to that aspect of their partner's nature that was ruled by the heart and what were known as "feelings"—provided that there was no betrayal of the idea that for both of them represented what was most important and ideally elevated in their life. But it is probable that this impersonal element in the relationship would often, between decent people, have led to "that sweet friendship, that tender confidence, which, joined to esteem, form, so it seems to me, the true and solid happiness of marriage" (as the hypocrite Madame de Merteuil, in an age that had lost respect for the idea of the family and that cultivated personal passion, with smooth-tongued falsity describes marriage). In any case, both would have realized that their relationship was indissoluble, just as their relationship to the king and country was in those times when feeling for these institutions was deep-rooted; indeed, it continued beyond the grave. They were united in coming generations of Rohans, or in the history of the family. Perhaps some of them might dream of being reunited with a more beloved spirit in Paradise, but in their tomb in the Rohan chapel they remained together in eternal rest within the imperishable marble.

Of course it can be said that all this applies to only a very limited number of families. But the presence of an elite is felt throughout the nation. The luster that shone from the relations between great families always illuminated the celebration of the marriage ceremony.

Nor was it any less sincere, even though less pompous, when a young clergyman married the young daughter of the vicarage, and two families were united who had been the guardians of Christianity in the country for centuries, or when an old yeoman family that had devotedly worked the beloved land for many generations acquired an excellent and decorous mistress for the people and animals on the farm, and a mother and grandmother for those who would take up their work there with renewed faithfulness . . . the highest feminine position that they were able to conceive of. Never mind that such concepts as feminine position and the sanctity of marriage may lose some of their luster when one is from Morbihan. There is no doubt that the farmer at Hill Farm—as long as respect for the family and the idea of property was deep and unquestioned—went to bed with his wife at Hill Farm with more solemnity and reverence than he could have shown any royal princess who had done him that honor.

Indeed, it may well be thought that in a country like Germany before the war, for instance, some of this luster could shine upon a whole nation's marriages and their task: to provide new Germans and raise them in the true faith. Or that in former days, when the human family represented the consciousness of being the children of God in the battle against natural forces and evil, the same luster might fall upon that task, of peopling the earth, and thus would make, so to speak, every love affair into a marriage.

But is it not asking too much of Candidate Petersen to expect him to feel something of her personality and of their personal love relationship symbolized abstractly in his young Mrs. Petersen, who went along with him one morning to the registry office, and with whom he shares a succession of different apartments and summer cottages, troubles with successive "maids" and tradesmen, a certain amount of unnecessary and tiresome socializing and utterly impersonal good works? Isn't it asking too much, not so much of his moral stamina as of his imagination, to expect him to see a radical difference between the child born to him and a pretty office girl before his marriage and his three legitimate children, the third of whom he and his wife hoped and tried to avoid?

Young Mrs. Petersen gave up her youth and vigor, as well as the time and talents that she previously (and as she now sometimes thinks with more appreciation) gave to her work, for the pleasure of living with Mr. Petersen and having a couple of dear little babies, whom she hopes will be able to make their way in life somehow or other. If the pleasure is now and again mixed, the whole enterprise may begin to seem somewhat dubious.

As a financial speculation—a viewpoint from which she has probably never considered it—it was dubious from the outset, for she had in fact felt freer and in a better position as a stenographer, and if she had had a free relationship with consequently only one child and the father's obligatory maintenance, she would have managed really well.

It is true that her children took his name, but she had herself been born a Petersen.

No wonder that this young married couple look back on their engagement as the most satisfactory period of their relationship, while for the duc and duchesse de Rohan this time held nothing at all apart from its promises.

The charm factor in Mr. and Mrs. Petersen's marriage is that of a free relationship, and it has not been raised to any higher plane, but has only been allotted some of the significance that a free love relationship, a purely personal relationship, finds it hard to uphold.

On that evening of May 1 when, as a young engaged couple, they rode out to Grib Lake on a motorcycle and smoked a cigarette by the shore while a nightingale started to sing in the beech forest behind them, while for once they felt they were quite alone in the whole world, and life seemed to have neither past nor future . . . then they felt themselves to be something real and their relationship something real.

Could not this quality and this reality have been more cherished, and were they not justified in sadly and reproachfully asking family and society, and themselves: "What actually is it, and what good does it do, that they have sacrificed themselves for?"

But the time of the family is past, and cannot be recalled. Nor would it be recalled even if this were possible. Many generations have given their thought and strength in order to annihilate it. We read of the values that its concept may have contained with a certain wistfulness, just as at the Château de Chambord, "the Voitures de Gala which were prepared in 1873 for the royal entrance of the comte de Chambord in Paris may be seen for 1 franc extra per person."

St. Christopher must turn away from the past and look to the present or the future.

## X. . . . . *Continues His Wanderings*

People in general have a somewhat confused understanding of the idea of truth.

Many people interpret truth in a negative sense: the person who does not lie tells the truth. So they go to their grave without ever having told a lie and without any idea at all of what truth is.

Others think that truth is best practiced as a kind of mental and emotional communism. The person who wishes to be truthful in relation to another must keep nothing to himself, but must reveal everything as well as demand to know everything. Truth cannot be fully achieved before people know all about each other's childhood love affairs and toothaches in detail. The true friend, son, husband has not a single corner of his soul that he can call his own, no possession that he has not shared out among the commune, and he feels that a secret is not a sweetness in the soul but a weight on his conscience.

This type of search for truth is practiced particularly in the home, and Danish art, which on the whole has paid homage to such a form of truth, has glorified it in many hundreds of interiors: the husband reading, with his pipe or his glass of toddy beside him, the elder children at their lessons, drinking milk and tea and eating their bread and butter, the wife nursing the youngest child, all gathered around the same lamp, while the dog, stretched out on the carpet, contributes to the intimate atmosphere of the home.

When our homes still surround themselves with an aura of ideality, indeed, regard themselves as the nation's greatest treasure, it is perhaps because they feel themselves to be the upholders of this particular type of truth . . . related to the type of love of truth and real intimacy that in the old days furnished "the smallest room" snugly enough with a row of seats, one beside the other, where a gathering of good friends might sit and discuss their mutual affairs in peace and quiet.

They plead this love of truth as one of their worthiest qualities, and maintain that one of the corrupting aspects of free love affairs is that a mistress makes use of her wiles and her attraction to hold on to her lover out of necessity (oh dear, oh dear, these poor old aging mistresses—*quote*), instead of appearing before him truthfully as she would be able to do if she were a legitimate wife with the law on her side, and so had no need to fear being weighed and found wanting. Many wedded wives bring to mind this creed, because in their homes one cannot help thinking what an almost divine change it would be for their husbands if they were suddenly caused to realize that their position was not at all as secure as they had thought, and that they would have to make some effort to keep it.

In reality, long unbroken cohabitation is probably a dangerous situation in which to practice such truth and intimacy, and there is something to be said for the old rule that "the nightdress is taken off for the lover, but kept on for the husband."

A pair of lovers can and must discard the last garment because their meetings are purely beautiful, in the mood for love. But even the most enamored couple, who intend to continue their relationship for the rest of their lives, ought to consider that sooner or later in the course of so long a time circumstances will arise that will make it preferable to retain a minimum of covering, and that it is not an especially attractive moment when they are obliged to dress again. It is easier to add to the truth and frankness within a relationship than to curtail it once it has been introduced, and the old habit of spouses using the formal manner of addressing each other probably had the same effect sometimes as the sort of cool atmosphere in which goods keep well without much deterioration.

It is not easy to accommodate oneself to cold comfort, and no doubt in the homes of former times they found, as King Frederik VI experienced, that "pillows were hard right from the cradle." But looked at from the viewpoint of mental hygiene, perhaps both these aspects had their good sides. The homes in which the young people of today are prepared for life, and which are completely devoid of any underlying idea at all (apart from the dogma of the sanctity of the home in itself), can often be compared to a nice soft bed. It cannot be denied, of course, that there is much to be said for this, for it gives rest to the weary, and is a solace for the sick and the overburdened. But it is not something to idealize; rather, it may be said that the briefer time one can with impunity stay in it the better. Neither is the nostalgia for it to be idealized, even though one can sympathize with it, but the homesickness that children who have been poisoned with self-pity feel and suffer can often be compared with a spoiled person's longing for his nice soft bed. Least of all is there anything to idealize in the custom of keeping fit people, who feel like getting up, in bed against their will . . . and yet how frequently that is the practice and is even idealized in homes where there are children and young people.

How often when one goes into one of these idealized homes does one get the same feeling, morally and intellectually, that strikes one physically in a crowded carriage or waiting room, where the windows are closed: the air is stale.

What one breathes in is the harmonically blended breath exhaled from the assembly, right down to the jokes now turned to dust that were new when the paterfamilias was a boy, and the taste of his favorite books that are stuffed into the younger generation like infinitely ancient cakes that it is no longer possible to digest or make use of as nourishment.

This is where many proud men have been boiled down into bread and milk, and many lovely young women have ended up with their whole family in a mutual mental cannibalism that has left them all with nothing but their bones; or parents and children have similarly suffered as would be the case where a mother kept her children at the breast until they were quite big, tearfully confronting anyone who tried to save either mother or child from being worn out or undernourished with the sanctity of mother's milk.

Where self-righteous people live together in a home that is not borne up by any idea at all except the dogma of the sanctity of that home, their self-righteousness will not only be increased but multiplied. Then they will end up by "becoming persuaded even unto unconsciousness that no one can even dwell under their roof without deep cause for thankfulness. Their children, their servants, must be fortunate ipso facto that they are theirs. . . ." In such a setting, the moral evaluation of other people will be decided solely in relation to their own evaluation of this holy home and the blessed society dwelling in it: that is to say that they, who know that Mama is wonderful and Papa unique, and Beech Grove the loveliest place in the world, are nice people, whereas the others are either stupid or nasty, or one does not reckon with them as people at all, and takes no interest in their existence.

As a preparation for life these blessed homes resemble the dancing school in *Emmeline,* where the girls learned the steps of the minuet like this: "three chassés forward toward the mirror, a pas de basque in front of the console table . . ." The Beech Grove children have no idea of how to act or conduct themselves anywhere but within the material and spiritual walls of Beech Grove, and therefore have good reason to look back on Beech Grove as the only place where they could live and come into their own —and the Beech Grove parents are proud of and moved by this.

When an institution in itself, without any underlying idea and without cause, is declared to be sanctified, then it is in truth time to open one's eyes and prepare an unbiased judgment. Just you come here, you homes demanding that a personal longing and passion shall be sacrificed for the sake of your sanctity, be honest for once and do not invoke the few homes that are ideal (any more than the few holy popes can be cited in defense of the infallibility of the pope or the papacy as a whole), but teach us in what it consists.

You are forgiven at the outset for not having been the mainstay of intellect or art, for not having been hearths where the holy fire could burn, for you were not capable of that. But you are not forgiven for having grudgingly prevented and condemned any striving after those things, because they were outside your domestic sphere and could put you in the shade . . . as could those friendships and infatuations in children and young people that seemed to you to be heresies against your holy orthodoxy.

Ah, have you not often been satisfied with not practicing any other kind of love than that expressed in the kiss of thanks for the meal with which "man and wife wipe each other's mouths instead of using a napkin," any other kind of sympathy than that by which elderly parents who want to excel and be admired in the easiest way force or accustom their children, under their guidance, to play more idiotic games than they would find out for themselves, and thereby persuade healthy children to be infantile—no other development than marking time, no other mission than self-worship? But only to be the prophets and agents of holy matrimony in such a way that will bring about half the number of new marriages because the bride wanted to leave home!

People who go to the theater do after all expect to hear something either amusing or gripping or touching, and in social life those with the right ideas of what is becoming between host and guests try to be at their intellectual best. It is only in home life that an assembly of people sit each with their book or newspaper or Patience yawning the time away until they can go to bed, and call this yawning a sacred ritual.

The fact that if there were to be a vote on the sanctity of the home, many pious voices would still be on its side, is of no consequence, for an established sanctity without any underlying idea and foundation is possessed of particular tenacity. When Ewald wrote:

> O misery, now carry to its rest,
> Ye men of the North,
> Bury its greatest treasure

no doubt he sang from a heart full of sincerity that found a sincere echo in the hearts of the people. So perhaps the people can recover from their sorrow over the sanctity of the home, just as in their time they got over their grief for King Frederik V.

## XI. Intermezzo

The *Edda* says that when the world is destroyed at Ragnarok, the gods will find the golden dice they played with in the morning of time in the grass of the plains of Ida.

So it seemed to the old Norsemen who fought a constant battle with grim necessity, with wind and weather, cold and crop failure, with bloody strife at home and abroad, with uncertainty and discomfort in all the conditions of life . . . as if the greatest happiness imaginable from any source that would last forever was simply this: to play.

And it is perhaps this same idea of bliss as an endlessly continuing game that has made the saying "No one can enter the kingdom of heaven without first becoming a child again" so popular among all nations.

What is under discussion here is not the kind of game in which those taking part make up everything out of their own imagination, by visualizing or making themselves believe in a danger or a goal—for this kind presupposes the existence of or memory of other "real" conditions, and would be impossible to play after Ragnarok. . . . Rather it is the kind of game that is sufficient in its own real charm or boldness, yet that dissociates itself from earthly life and resembles something generally more associated with a heavenly state, as it is not subject to the strict laws of necessity but its own divinely intelligent ones, and a spirit of goodwill and harmony is assumed among all the participants and through all vicissitudes.

In old Danish, and most other languages, the same word was used to define playing games and playing, for instance, a musical instrument, or cards, or for acting or dancing, to which all the same laws applied, or in older times for fighting in tournaments, not much less dangerous than war itself and in which there was no less opportunity to show bravery and contempt of death, but for which such rules were evolved as the knights themselves could have wished to apply in war and in which no real hatred or enmity was present.

So one can imagine the possibility that as humanity gradually relieved itself of the heavy yoke of "the ferocious necessity, mistress of men and gods," all the phenomena of life would come to be regarded or accepted in this way, and that then love between a man and a woman would represent the most beautiful and bold thing in life, its best game.

One cannot say what it would be like to live under such conditions, for no real attempt has been made to realize them. There was far too much against it to make it feasible: on the one hand the fear of heaven and hell, and on the other, far too much uncertainty in all earthly relationships—"earnestness" had a right to see far too much danger and light-mindedness in all such games, and, speaking broadly, to call them sinful.

The attempts of the ladies and lovers of the age of chivalry to make this game a reality resulted in a great flowering of love poetry and art—indeed, probably most of that charm surrounding love that still delights us today—but in the rough and fierce and uncertain centuries there was far too much against it for it to be really true. And just as King Francis I believed that he had learned "all the laws of the divine game," from the other side of the Atlantic there came a grim shadow that put an end to the whole game for King Francis himself. The eighteenth century achieved a certain perfection in its game with this "stuff of nature that the power of imagination has embroidered," and knew "a harmony between desire and satisfaction that modern yearning never possesses" . . . but it could only be played by a very small, privileged section of society, and the shadow of the poverty and battles of the great mass of the people rose up against it and engulfed it.

It may well be said that it is up to and during the present time that these two shadows—in addition to that dark shadow of responsibility for the welfare of the coming generations, which seems to interfere with the life of love with such arbitrariness and fatefulness—when the shadow of the fear of hell shrunk and grew less, have done most to throw gloom over the game of love in life, and most often turned it into grim earnest. The Devil himself, illness, financial worries and <u>uncontrolled births</u> have been far too heavy burdens for humanity ever to have been able to realize this: to see love in its life as it does, for instance, art, as its highest "delight."

With so much that was serious at risk it might well seem —as has generally been represented—as if the partner in a love relationship who was serious must always take precedence over the one for whom it was a game. When one partner could accuse, "You have been playing with me," the other could plead no defense from the moral point of view.

But gradually, as it seems possible for these shadows to lift one by one, we may see the time come when the partner so accused will be able to reply: "Yes, I have been playing with you because the best side of my nature reveals itself in play, and play is sacred. But you, you poor wretch, you were mean and unyielding in spirit, you did not understand how to play. Go and work or preach and keep away from love, for where it is concerned you are like a musician with no sense for music, or one who is afraid of intoxication where wine is drunk."

In all fairness it must probably be said that throughout the ages it is men who consciously or unconsciously have tried to maintain this view, and that it has been mainly the women who have taken a serious view of things, and have tried, where they could, to make men take love seriously too. For most past generations of men—whose understanding of these things was not completely controlled by their women—it was their work, war, ideas, the family that they took seriously, while love to them was pleasure and play.

But there has been some inequality here, and women were not in a position where they could play, even when they had a predisposition to do so. It might still have been possible in those societies and periods in which marriage was the concern of the clan, the family or society, and was arranged by them—in the same way that the family, the home and work represented life in earnest to the woman, and love in itself had no place there— as is still the case in old-fashioned society in the Latin nations, or among the Arabs, for instance, from whom the crusader knights are said to have taken their first ideas of love as a game and an art.

But in a situation where the whole future, position, indeed life of women was entirely dependent on their love relationships in a completely different way from that of their men—as for instance for the last century in England and the whole of northern Europe—then one could hardly expect them to have a sense of play. Zarathustra might well point out to them that "in every man there hides a child who wants to play. Come then, you women, and find the child in man." This would seem a risky idea to someone who knew that the whole life, welfare and property of herself and her children were utterly dependent on that child.

And throughout all ages and societies, woman's physical contribution to a love relationship—whether, so to speak, she would or no—made it an extremely serious matter for her.

Many, many love affairs and marriages all through the ages have deteriorated and become embittered through this unequal situation.

From the purely practical point of view it might be arranged that men divided themselves among two sides of the feminine personality, and "had wedded wives to run our houses and bear us legitimate children, and hetairai to teach us the joys of love."

This was probably quite a workable arrangement, for the women as well, who after all could generally choose according to their taste whether they would be ladies of pleasure or nannies. And you might say that if the men had had a spark of good sense, they would have made every effort to maintain this state of things.

But almost all the slavery in the world has been—albeit not always consciously—abolished from above. For the slaveowner is unsatisfied and demands slaves with a sense of responsibility, or wives who can sing for him and entertain his friends, or mistresses with whom he can discuss his business affairs. Apart from those with the most primitive natures, perhaps average men would have found that their house was not run as they might have wished, or that the joys of love in which they were instructed did not bring them long-lasting happiness, or that their children's beauty or talents were not what they had hoped for. And hereby there developed, quite slowly, the phenomenon that took shape and outraged the world in the last century, which was called the emancipated woman.

She came at a serious time, and was therefore obliged to behave seriously in order to be taken seriously. Perhaps, too, an instinct that has taken centuries to develop is the hardest thing of all for the liberated to liberate themselves from. Young liberated women were prepared to give as good as they got, for now was the moment when the world was to feel the effect of woman's hard-tried moral sense. Men's ideals of love had in the past done her much harm and little good, and now, when she was no longer the plaything of love but a comrade in work and striving, now most of all love, whether it be free or bound, was to be taken seriously.

But force of circumstances brought a change in her, even before she had changed her program. In the softer air of freedom she herself, after a couple of generations, came to take everything more easily. Now her grand-daughters, mentally and physically independent, are their young men's playmates in these postwar years.

They do not seem to be quite sure of the game yet. There is still to this day a certain amount of hissing and scratching in protest at the rule applying to all games, that no one must "lose their temper," but the loser and the winner must shake hands without rancor. To educate the next generation, we might need a court and school of love like that of the comtesse de Provence of old, where young people learned discipline in affairs of the heart and were taught courtesy, boldness and sophistication in love.

Much is demanded of those who are to be really proficient at play. Courage and imagination, humor and intelligence, but in particular that blend of unselfishness, generosity, self-control and courtesy that is called *gentilezza*. Alas, there has been so little demand and exercise of this in love affairs. So many excellent men and women have demanded it of themselves in relation to their circles of acquaintances and subordinates, but in their marriages have thought that they had every possible right to be egoistic, uncontrolled, jealous . . . for where love was concerned, it was not really an ideal.

And yet it is play's own spirit, true *gentilezza,* that there is most need of in human love affairs, and that has most power, the minute it appears, to idealize them—whether they are to last for a day or for all eternity.

Those who love to play are constantly being criticized for being superficial . . . and not least where love is concerned.

"Yes," they can reply, "we are superficial in the same way as a ship sailing across the sea. We do not consider it any advantage to reach the bottom, for at best that is what is known as going aground."

Those violent passions that take themselves so "seriously" cannot run a smooth course. The life they create is like that of the pendulum and they result in reactions, indeed, in total impotence.

But it is easy to imagine a game going on throughout eternity, like the games of the Aesir on the plains of Ida, as Shelley imagines it in *Prometheus Unbound*. When the fearful sufferings of humanity are at an end and the forces of tyranny have been cast into the abyss by the Demogorgon, then will all human passions

> . . . in life's green grove
> sport like tame beasts, none knew how gentle
> they could be!

## XII. The Heavy Child: A Fantasy

King Louis XVI wrote in his diary: "14/7 1789: Nothing." And it is very possible that if Pilate had kept a diary, he would have written in it on the night of Good Friday: "Nothing. Slight earthquake just before dinner." Yes, God help us, this is how we all keep diaries, for it requires unusual superiority to take in what is right in front of our noses.

Perhaps this is how the historians of humanity will record the first twenty-five years of the twentieth century and will note: "Airplanes, the Great War, revolutions and Bolshevism," ignorant of the fact that an idea has seen the light of day from which quite different revolutions will grow, a new religion has been established or practiced, and not write down in their history: "It was during these years that the idea of birth-control and eugenics was first mooted and consolidated."

It is disturbing to think that many times this really is what happens; it is disturbing to think of good-natured King Louis seating himself in his bedroom at Versailles, taking thought and writing his few words, and think that from that day on the ground trembled beneath his feet and shook the fat powdered head on his shoulders. It is disturbing to think that now we take part in small arguments as to whether the discussion of "birth-control" is decent or indecent, and that the idea of it is present in the consciousness and way of thinking of young people here, there, and everywhere, and is accepted by families with a sigh of relief, as a gift, a mercy, quite simply, to smooth the rough path of life, while perhaps it really means that now a tremendous demand is being made on humanity from which it can never again release itself, a great burden has been placed on our shoulders.

After St. Christopher had searched for a long time for someone stronger than himself whom he might serve, he finally settled down to the job of carrying travelers across a river. One day a small child came and asked to be carried across, and Reprobus set him on his shoulders. But as they went deeper out into the water, the child grew heavier and heavier, and when they were halfway across he staggered under the weight and turned to reproach the child for putting his life in danger. Then the child began to speak and said: "Be not afraid of my weight, Reprobus, for on your shoulders you bear him who made the world and sustains it."

Now, we cannot tell whether this really reassured Reprobus. One would think that he could not possibly have been told anything that would have terrified him more, just at the moment when he was staggering about in the middle of the river. But at least now his search was over and he had found one who was strong enough for him and whom he could serve with all his heart.

To return to the problem of love and of ideality in love and love relationships, and to sum up all these observations: the considered opinion must be that a love affair is ideal to the degree that the individuals feel that they are in contact with and are influenced by their highest ideals.

Thus, when the clan and the family were the highest things in life, the ideal love relationships were those that served the clan and the family, that is to say, the lawful marriages, in which a wife bore her husband many children.

Thus, at the time when the practice of a certain religion, the Church, and the future life in Paradise were the highest ideals in life, then (although all earthly circumstances were in themselves open to doubt) the love affair that enjoyed the blessing of the Church, that was perfectly in accordance with the spirit and discipline of the Church, was the most ideal.

But it is hypocritical, superficial and immoral, it is altogether wrong and unreasonable to attempt to idealize a love relationship with rules and formulae from those ideals that no longer are ideal and no longer have any real life. They are salt that has lost its power, and no matter how much of that kind of salt orthodoxy uses, it will not stop the rot.

Therefore, to an artist, for whom his art is the highest thing, that love relationship and the mistress who gives him inspiration are great and noble; but the things under whose influence his art declines in quality are the opposite of ideal.

Therefore, to the present young generation, who prize individualism above all else, who see love as the highest thing in human life, and whose ideals, when they have any, are freedom and beauty, every love affair that can be conducted freely and beautifully and in which the personalities can understand, help, give joy to each other has every possibility of existing ideally in itself, without any external enlightenment.

Therefore, when people take up eugenics in earnest, the love that collaborates in this will be judged as the ideal.

Then it will really have discovered something stronger than itself that it can serve with enthusiasm and that does not, like the ruler of Canaan, fear the Devil, or, like the Devil himself, fear the Cross. In the middle of the river it will acquire the strength to bear its burden in the consciousness of its enormous importance and extent.

Throughout the ages human beings have constantly striven to widen their horizons, the area of their interdependence and interest. It spread from the home, the family and the clan to the class and the nation. Now, while the concept of patriotism is still not a century old, humanity surely has courage and imagination enough to take the huge step of encompassing the race itself, the whole of humanity, with the same feeling of responsibility, the same burning desire to serve.

And people will widen their horizon, as far as time is

concerned. They must come to reckon with a completely new yardstick for temporality and eternity.

Both past and future are, to an unlimited extent in the family and the race, present in the individual and the present. A thousand families have blended their blood in the single individual, and he can, in coming generations, extend his influence over the life of the race for a thousand years into the future.

It is reasonable to suppose that when the sense of interdependence, of unity as a race, has penetrated human consciousness, a person will be evaluated far more for his extraction and his "blood" than at present, just as is the case with individual specimens of purebred animals.

Now, it is sometimes said that it takes three generations to produce a "gentleman," and against this very modest demand other opinions maintain that ten or twenty years of educating the individual will suffice. Coming generations will probably work with quite different periods of time, with gentlemen of ten, twenty, fifty generations, and people in general will be assessed according to events that have taken place, circumstances that have occurred, many generations before their birth. What Samuel Butler wrote fifty years ago will be generally acknowledged: "If a man is to enter the Kingdom of Heaven he must do so, not only as a little child, but as a little embryo, or rather as a little zoosperm—and not only this, but as one that has come of zoosperms which have entered into the Kingdom of Heaven before him for many generations . . . postnatal accidents are not, as a rule, so permanent in their effect. . . ." Or, to cite another English author, that humanity has made a great error in "seizing on a certain moment, no more intrinsically notable than any other moment, and [has] called it Birth. The habit of honouring one single instant of the universal process to the disadvantage of all other instants has done more, perhaps, than anything to obfuscate the crystal clearness of the fundamental flux."

It requires no laws and rules to practice such a philosophy of life. They will be innate in the consciousness in the same way as are present-day moral laws, and no decent person will be able to avoid them.

Naturally this kind of feeling of responsibility for the welfare of the stock already exists to a certain extent, but as long as all the old superstitions surrounding marriage and external laws still held sway the whole matter was in a fine state of confusion. The immorality of bringing illegitimate children into the world was assessed by thinking people, after some of the splendor had faded from the magical formula of the wedding ceremony, according to their homelessness and lack of family; but closely related persons were free to marry and bring large families of second-rate specimens into the world, or people of mixed races could produce, naturally also under the sacred sign of marriage, children with much less possibility of leading a normally successful life than a healthy illegitimate child—even when homeless and without a family—without offending against morality.

Presumably in the future only one category of "illegitimate" children will be reckoned with, in the same way as "false" coinage is reckoned with—that is, those who in some way or other do not possess full value as human beings, and whom it will not benefit the race to pay full value for.

To make these part of the stock in trade will perhaps be regarded as not merely immoral but criminal, even more than it is nowadays considered criminal just to remove an individual from its stock. Future Sherlock Holmeses will then be able to concentrate their talents on and make their exciting reports on the tracking down and just punishment of such criminals.

But it is not the criminal law—it is never the criminal law —that in any way at all will decide the issue. It is, of course, conscience, and that is an inescapable fact.

It must have been a very serious matter for those who in their time had gone to the greatest possible lengths to purchase from the Church indulgences for their departed and who then later encountered Luther, and whether they would or no came to feel that he was right. It was not only that their peace of mind in the conviction of having done the right thing was shaken and dissolved, and their merits shrunk to nothing, but that from then on there seemed to be no end to the demands made on them if they wanted to go to heaven. The more they thought of them, the worse they grew, for eternal bliss for themselves and their families appeared to be impossible to attain through any outward means at all, but here was this dreadfully energetic German impressing on them that even more was needed, indeed, that only by giving the very greatest possession of all, their whole personality, would they be giving enough. For very superficial people this might have come as a relief, a saving of money, time and effort, in the same way as the system of birth-control does; but serious folk would totter and faint under the burden.

If human beings should really come to accept the view that their own future and their eternal salvation lie in their own hands —that the indulgences of the Church and society in the form of marriage certificates are only "scraps of paper," and all their great merits in having secured homes and schools and perhaps a substantial fortune for their descendants amount to very little—then they will be confronted with an even greater responsibility. For the eternal salvation of the individual must then always be his own affair, and he could not through slovenliness drag others, certainly not an unlimited number of other human beings, with him into hell. Every young couple would be like Adam and Eve in the Garden of Eden looking ahead to innumerable generations, knowledgeable in the wisdom of eugenics as Adam and Eve were not, and clear in the realization that they possess the possibility of bringing suffering or joy to thousands for thousands of years.

It may well be that where love itself and the position of love relationships in society are concerned, free love affairs will be tolerated as long as they do not burden the race with undesirable specimens. And regarded according to whether they are, for instance, the inspiration for ideal works or activities, or form a center for art or science or philanthropy, or merely are attractive to their fellows as examples of beautiful and happy relationships, they will be the private concern of individuals in the same way that a friendship is now, in whose course and conclusion no one else is concerned. Society will come to accept that moral values have moral heirs and are not dependent on the flesh.

But will the elite of society be left in peace in this kind of limited and personal relationship? Will not the whole of society beg them even more fervently than Shakespeare begged and implored his beloved and admired Mr. W. H. to "make thee another self for love of me," and impress upon them that

No love towards others in such bosom sits
That on himself such murderous shame commits. . . .

And will not racial conscience threaten their own hearts just as in the old story the shadows of unborn generations threatened the woman who, from indolence and fear of sorcery, had fought shy of having children?

Now what would this lead to? What would it be like in a society that went in for marriage with this idea in mind?

Of course, only a prophet could make more than a fairly idle guess. But at least the written word cannot be importunate —anyone who thinks it is completely useless has no need to read on.

One could, for instance, discuss whether it is probable that it would lead to monogamy. Many people feel that the constant striving involved in love affairs has been working toward this goal. To begin with, this is an extremely dubious assumption in itself, and even if it should really be the case, it would prove absolutely nothing where further development is concerned, for a constant striving continuing through many centuries may suddenly, after having reached its culmination point, be completely reversed. Thus a citizen living in 1700 would believe that society had worked continuously toward autocracy and was then very close to its goal, while in reality the complete (and lasting) overthrow of autocracy was only a few years away. In a society where the object of marriage was the improvement of the race, there would be a good deal to be said against monogamy, because "the maternal instinct leads a woman to prefer a tenth share in a first-rate man to the exclusive possession of a third-rate one."

Moreover, one would think that the definite requirement for the ideality of a marriage—the bettering of the race—would upset another apparently continuous striving in the development, namely, the demand for equal moral evaluation of man and woman in love relationships, and that this would be based on the naturally unequal proportion as regards the number of children a father or mother can naturally bring into the world. If it did not sound so crude to compare human beings and animals in this respect, it would be most suitable to take examples from, for instance, the improvement of breeds of horses, where it would be considered highly immoral if not criminal to allow a blood mare of pure stock, who had won the Derby, to give birth to a half-blooded foal—not to speak of a mule—but not to let her brother do his bit to ennoble the half-blooded stock.

The sort of marriage that is extremely common today, where the wife is mentally and physically far superior to her husband, would in future, from the viewpoint of the ideal improvement of the race, seem reprehensible in the highest degree, because a husband of equal birth or only slight superiority could easily give her those children that she had the time and the strength to give birth to with the greatest benefit to the race, but which is not at all the case with her present brood. (And the advantages that the bad husband she now has can give her in the sphere of money and position would not be permitted to play any part here, where great ideals were what mattered.) Here one would be in the position of Mohammedan society, where parents are not allowed to give their daughter to a man of humbler birth, since the women, on account of their great value as potential mothers, on principle always marry above themselves. In the society of the future this would not be maintained by means of laws or rules; it would be consciously recognized as the requirement for each decent person to make a decent relationship.

In the end it seems possible that science—which by that time would really know something about marriage and heredity—might come to the conclusion that there was truth in the old dogma that love children are the finest specimens (that at least would make the judgment of the superior morality of old-style marriage inapplicable; we should hear no more from that quarter).

How eagerly then would society be on the lookout for a

really personal passion, and a so-called crazy love affair would rank at once among the forces that work for the edification of society! How loudly would the voices of duty and conscience thunder in the ears of those who out of habit or indolence or fear then neglect the opportunity to blend beauty and strength in the life of the race!

Paolo and Francesca would have their place between the most august members of society and the martyrs, and the prophet Nathan would chastise Uriah, who had not the moral and ideal strength to yield when it was a question of producing a King Suleiman ben Daoud.

"Well, and will all this be the least bit better or happier?" ask the protagonists of the old marriage, and the old free love.

It could easily be imagined to be happier, if happiness were understood as the feeling of satisfaction and well-being—if it were principally the happy type of person who was selected to continue the human race. Mazarin said that he could only care for happy people, and if this was his main principle in the choice of those around him, it would be bound to have the result that his circle of acquaintances and surroundings quickly grew happier. If the ideal of humanity was to be happy, and it was able to decide to put everything into being so, it is at least possible that it could succeed in creating a race that could be happy and the kind of conditions in which it could be happy. But it is not impossible that if a vote were taken regarding this decision, the majority would opine that to have an ideal is happiness.

And this ideal now? No idealist would object to its demanding enormous sacrifices, any more than St. Christopher could object to a child's supernatural weight on his shoulders, since that was how it first revealed its divinity. But he could perhaps have reason, or the right, to ask if it were incontrovertibly the strongest, and if it might not be possible that he would at some time be confronted with something even stronger which even the one he now carried and served would come to fear or bow down before.

With infinitude on every side no one can find an answer to this question. But there is one piece of advice to give a modern St. Christopher, and that is: If he sees someone stronger, then serve him.

In its constant striving for growth, for the ability to grasp as much as possible, humanity can surely reach further, find something greater than itself.

For those nations that were—or still are, as in the case of the Somalis—divided up into mutually hostile tribes, it seems unreasonable and unnatural to this day that they should ever be able to be united under one national banner. And to the burning patriots of the last generation it seemed quite impossible that they should feel anything for humanity in general, or fraternity for any other than a countryman.

And yet love of clan has undoubtedly grown out of love of family and home, love of country out of love for clan, and the idea of the brotherhood of all humanity has arisen the stronger from the fearful flames the love of country burst out into.

The human beings of the future, who will not have the slightest difficulty in comprehending the fourth dimension—and this will undoubtedly not take long if we start on it straightaway —and who have consciously taken the work of development out of the hands of nature and said to it: "My will be done, not thine," will then perhaps be able enthusiastically to merge into an even higher unity and embrace a larger brotherhood with the same enthusiasm as that with which Habr Yunis meets Habr

Yunis, and with which the patriots of the forties sang to and embraced the children of their beloved common fatherland.

So with these fantasies must these observations, begun in all modesty, end.

No one can know what he is in for when he embarks on a search for the strongest . . . nor where he may end up when he begins to talk about it.

# Notes to "On Modern Marriage and Other Observations"

## BY ELSE CEDERBORG

*Page 32*  ON MODERN MARRIAGE AND OTHER OBSERVATIONS, an essay in twelve chapters, was written in 1923–24 as Karen Blixen's reply to her younger brother, Thomas Dinesen (1892–1979), in their continuous discussion about sexual morals. It was first published by the Karen Blixen Society in *BLIXENIANA 1977* (Copenhagen, Denmark). Thomas stayed with his sister for long periods when she was a farmer in Kenya in 1913–31 (cf. p. 7), and even for a while considered buying a farm himself. In November 1920 he came to assist her in sorting out the tangled economic situation at the farm, and to obtain information for the family limited company that held the shares in this African enterprise. As he did not go back to Denmark until March 2, 1923, they had good opportunities for discussions, and some of these Blixen touched upon in her letters to their mother, Ingeborg Dinesen (1856–1939), as can be seen from the edited collection of letters: *Letters from Africa 1914– 1931* (published in English in 1981). For instance, on March 25, 1922, she writes:

Thomas is not suited to being out here; this is absolutely clear to me, although I would find it difficult to define why.—Thomas is not practical and has no interest in practical matters; I think that his talents lie much more in the direction of theoretical science, of almost any and every kind.—It is these long discussions that I hate with all my heart that actually interest him more than anything else, and I feel that I am a *bore* for him when I keep returning to oxen and plowing and the most prosaic kind of calculations. [p. 125]

Now and then she may have been annoyed by these discussions, but she must also have missed them—and her brother—because only a few months after he leaves for Denmark she starts working on *On Modern Marriage and Other Observations.* In a letter to her mother dated November 11, 1923, she writes: "Thomas will probably be glad to hear that I am writing a little piece on sexual morality, if only I can get it finished. Actually Thomas and I could never agree over that question." [p. 175]

The letters to Ingeborg Dinesen show us how the essay is progressing slowly and painstakingly over the months. On December 29, 1923, she writes to her mother:

During the Christmas period I tried to make use of the time to work on my paper about "sexual morality" for Tommy; but I find that I am having to restrict the subject somewhat and it will rather be about marriage, and I am writing with some trepidation as Tommy has always accused me of being reactionary. It is actually very difficult to write about this kind of thing when one is quite alone and also without access to the books from which one would like to quote, so I will probably never get very far with it. I grew so cross over not getting on better with it that I stopped working at literature in order to teach Hassan to make croustades, with more success. [p. 181]

Even though she complains of not having the books she needs to quote from, she managed all the same, as she seems to have quoted or paraphrased from memory when she had no other options. This, of course, often makes it more or less impossible to establish the source.

On May 22, 1924, the first eight chapters were sent to Thomas in Denmark, and on June 20 they were followed by the remaining four. *Letters from Africa 1914–1931* contains only Karen Blixen's own letters, so that we do not have Thomas's comments on his sister's long essay, but we can see that their discussion continued. As they were very close, he was the one to whom she turned whenever she wanted support or simply to pour out her heart.

However, some of the very finest letters on the subjects that were treated in *On Modern Marriage and Other Observations,* such as marriage, sexual morals, new lifestyles, and so on, were written to Karen Blixen's maternal aunt, Mary Bess Westenholz (1857–1947), a devout Unitarian and feminist. Blixen also discussed these matters with her younger sister, Ellen Dahl (1886–1959), and with her mother, though to a lesser degree. For instance, she tells her mother her opinion of the new lifestyles when the older woman gets upset about what are called "Tommy's flirtations." On January 27, 1924, Karen writes to her mother:

—in my opinion it is quite certain that the young
men and girls of the present generation see
themselves as completely equal in all situations of
importance. This is particularly true where erotic
relationships are concerned, which has of necessity
brought about changes in these, and views on them,
to a considerable extent.—The most significant thing
of all is probably this: that a girl is no longer
disparaged in her own or in a young man's eyes
through a love affair. [pp. 187–189]

Obviously this has a certain bearing on the subject of
*On Modern Marriage and Other Observations,* but there are
several more direct comments on her work with it. In
another letter to her mother, also about "Tommy's flirtations," she writes (April 13, 1924):

My typewriter ribbon is rotten because I have been
writing away at my essay on marriage for Thomas,
—but I am not making any progress with it partly
because I have no one to discuss it with or to
criticize what I have written, so I do not know
whether it is not the most banal thing in the world,
and partly because I cannot verify quotations to use
as I have no books to consult. I am of the opinion
that in reality there is no longer any such thing as
marriage, or only in name, and that what has to be
done is, either reestablish it on some basis or other
that is clearly evolved,—or to teach people to
practice free love, which they have so to speak
jumped into completely unprepared for, with more
dignity and beauty. Personally I believe that a new
kind of marriage will be constructed on the idea of

race: *eugenics, birth control,* etc., with a stricter idealism than that of the old form, but that free love will be entitled to exist without restraint, to be people's private shaurie [Swahili for "nuisance," and "worry"]. There is no prestige at all left in present-day marriage; this is certainly the case, anyhow, among the English, and I do not myself think that a marriage that is not upheld by some religious, moral or social idea in some way, and that can be dissolved at any time, for instance because of a single case of infidelity,—and that is entered upon with this assumption by both partners,—deserves to carry any prestige or is worth preserving. [pp. 201–202]

In her letter to Thomas enclosing the last four chapters, she says that "the pagination is a bit muddled (2 × 69 and 2 × 77), which I hope is not confusing. I look forward greatly to hearing your opinion of it." At that time the work was named by its first chapter.

*Page 32*   CHARLES ROBERT DARWIN (1809–1882), the English naturalist and author. In his most famous work, *The Origin of Species by Natural Selection, or The Preservation of Favoured Races in the Struggle for Life* (1859), he posited the idea that the present host of animal life began from a few elemental forms. When these developed, certain types of animals propagated while others less suited to the battle of life died out. The most controversial part of this theory was the notion that humans had descended from apes.

*Page 32*   JEAN-BAPTISTE MONET DE LAMARCK (1774–1829), the French biologist who contended that plants and animals will develop the characteristics required for continued existence. In his *Philosophie zoologique* (1809) he enunciated his views on evolution as four laws, and of these the fourth expressed his belief in the inherited effects of use and disuse, or the inheritance of acquired characteristics.

*Page 35*    "be full of the devilment": originally French, "le diable au corps," i.e., to be extremely lively. This may also be a reference to the novel by R. Radiguet, *Le Diable au corps* (1923).

*Page 35*    "Contemptibles": the name of the British Expeditionary Force of about 150,000 men who in 1914 joined the French and Belgians against Germany. The name was chosen in defiance of the German Kaiser, who was said to have used it as a derogatory expression in an army order that same year.

*Page 37*    St. Peter's: St. Peter's Basilica in Rome, Italy, is considered the central church of Roman Catholicism. It is believed to have been built on the site of St. Peter's grave in Vatican City.

*Page 37*    Werther and Lotte: In the novel *The Sorrows of Young Werther* (1774), by Johann Wolfgang Goethe, Werther commits suicide for unrequited love for his friend's fiancée, Lotte.

*Page 37*    Nora is the heroine of *A Doll's House* (1879) by Henrik Ibsen. In the play, she leaves her conventional husband and their children when he fails to live up to her marital ideals.

*Page 38*    Sigurd and Brynhild: Sigurd is the Siegfried of the Volsunga Saga, the Scandinavian version of the *Niebelungen-*

*lied,* who falls in love with the Valkyrie Brynhild (Brunhild), but abandons her and marries Gudrun under the influence of a love potion.

*Page 38*     ROMEO AND JULIET are the very young lovers in the tragedy *Romeo and Juliet* (ca. 1595) by William Shakespeare. They are recognized as the epitome of romantic love.

*Page 38*     KLISTER AND MALLE: This older, very conventional couple have been engaged to get married for years without being able to do anything about it. They appear in *De Uadskillelige (The Inseparable,* 1827), by the Danish playwright and critic Johan Ludvig Holberg (1791–1860). "Klister" means glue, and "Malle" is the same as "eye" in "hook and eye." As a couple they symbolize a relationship between man and woman that has dried up from convention and habit.

*Page 38*     TOMBOY: originally French, "la garçonne." The fashionable woman of the 1920s, with short cropped hair and a very slim and boyish look, was called "la garçonne."

*Page 38*     JACK DEMPSEY, the American boxer who was world heavyweight champion in 1919–26. In 1921 the French boxer Georges Carpentier was knocked out by Dempsey in a heavyweight title fight in the United States.

*Page 39*     *DOUBT AND FAITH:* Danish, *Tvivl og Tro,* 1909, was written by the dean of Roskilde Cathedral in Denmark, H. Martensen-Larsen.

*Page 39*     "LOOP THE LOOP": airplane maneuver in which a plane, starting upwards, does a full vertical loop.

*Page 41*     HARALD THE FAIR: the Norwegian king Harald Hårfager (ca. 850–943), also called Harold Fairhair.

*Page 41*     LOUIS XIV: the absolute king of France in the years 1638–1715; also called the Sun King.

*Page 41*     AMALIENBORG PALACE: the royal palace in Copenhagen.

*Page 42*     "THOSE WHO CARRIED ITS FLAG": The first real fight for women's rights in Denmark led to the formation of Dansk Kvindesamfund (the Danish Women's Society) in 1871. These women wanted to keep the marriage institution and strongly opposed the idea of "free love" as it was broadcasted by left-wing men in the 1880s. The same men who dreamed of sexually liberated women often denied them equal rights in social affairs, and Dansk Kvindesamfund first and foremost fought for political and social changes in the position of women.

*Page 43*     "THE CONFUSION OF MARRIAGE . . . SINGLE ERROR": a quotation from *Man and Superman* (1903), Act III, by George Bernard Shaw, and said by the great seducer Don Juan in his conversation with the Statue and Ana.

*Page 51*     "IS TO STEP . . .": not identified.

*Page 51*     "AWESOME LIKE THE SIGHT . . .": originally French, "terrible comme l'aspect d'un étendard . . . et le charme de son regard, est un clairon qui nous entraine." The quotation has not been identified.

*Page 51*     "SOUL BECAME A SONG . . .": not identified.

*Page 52*     VENUS ANADYOMENE rising from the sea in a painting by the Greek painter Apelles (born ca. 370 B.C.), who was considered the greatest painter of antiquity.

*Page 52*     MOHAMMEDAN LAW: For Blixen's interpretation of the relationship between the Mohammedan man and woman, see Chapter III in Part III, "The Somali Women," in *Out of Africa.*

*Page 53*     "THE GREAT EMPEROR OTTO": a limerick. The meaning in this context is given by its consisting of two mottoes: "L'État c'est moi," French for "I am the State," the motto of Louis XIV (1638–1715); and "Ich dien," German for "I serve," the motto of the English Prince of Wales since the time of Edward, the Black Prince (1330–1376). In Welsh, "Eich dyn" means "Your Man," which gives the motto a double significance.

*Page 53*     KORMAK AND STENGERDE are the lovers in an Icelandic saga, *Kormak's Saga* (ca. 1200–1230), but the quotation is from the saga pastiche *Kormak og Stengerde (Cormak and Stengerde)* by the Danish author J. P. Jacobsen, which was published in his *Digte og Udkast (Poems and Drafts)* in 1886.

*Page 54*     FREJA: (Freyja) the old Nordic goddess of love, who in many respects resembles the Greek Aphrodite and the Roman Venus.

*Page 59*     CHRISTOPHER THE HOLY: probably from the third century. His name actually means "Christ-bearer," which gave rise to the legend that he was an immensely strong man who used to carry travelers across a river. He became the patron of all travelers, and was celebrated on July 25, but in

1969 his name was dropped from the official liturgical calendar.

*Page 59*   JACOBUS DE VORAGINE (or Varagine), also known as Jacobo da Varazze, who was born ca. 1228 and died in 1298, was an Italian theologian and hagiographer. The first edition of his *The Golden Legend* was published in 1470 in Latin.

*Page 59*   "ART FOR ART'S SAKE": originally French, "L'art pour l'art." This was the "war cry" of the so-called Parnassian School, the name given to a group of French poets flourishing in the 1860s with Leconte de Lisle as their leader. The expression was first coined by Théophile Gautier in the introduction to his novel *Mademoiselle de Maupin* (1835–36), and has been revived by various groups.

*Page 60*   THE ITALIAN BORGIA FAMILY was considered very adept at poisoning their enemies with tasty dishes. Two major offenders were the military and political adventurer Cesare Borgia (ca. 1475–1507), and his father, who became Pope Alexander VI in 1492.

*Page 64*   THE ENGLISH GENTLEMEN-THIEF A. J. RAFFLES was the hero in three short story collections and one novel by Ernest William Hornung (1866–1921). Even though Raffles is one of the greatest craftsmen in the literature of roguery, he never loses his charm or good manners.

*Page 66*   DE ROHAN, a noble French family from the Morbihan Department in western France, had a chapel erected on their estate in 1603. Their family history goes back to 1104.

*Page 67*   MADEMOISELLE DE ROHAN: Marie de Rohan-Montbazon (1600–1679) by her second marriage became the wife of

Claude de Lorraine, duc de Chevreuse, in 1622. She was known to engage in various political conspiracies against, e.g., the chief minister of France, Cardinal Jules Mazarin.

*Page 68*     "THAT SWEET FRIENDSHIP . . .": Madame de Merteuil is the villain of the novel *Les Liaisons dangereuses* (*Dangerous Acquaintances,* 1782) by the French writer P.-A.-F. Choderlos de Laclos. The quotation is from her hypocritical letter to Madame de Volanges of October 4, 17$^{xx}$: "[and habit, which fortifies all inclinations which it does not destroy, brings about, little by little,] cette douce amitié, cette tendre confidence, qui, jointes à l'estione, forment le véritable, le solide bonheur des mariages" (from the translation into English by Ernest Dowson, London, 1940).

*Page 69*     MORBIHAN: the French department where the Rohan family lived. Cf. note to page 66.

*Page 69*     FARMER AT HILL FARM: the ordinary or even archetypal farmer.

*Page 71*     THE CHÂTEAU DE CHAMBORD (or castle of Chambord) was built by the French king Francis I in 1519–37. It has been considered a masterpiece in French Renaissance architecture.

*Page 71*     THE VOITURES DE GALA: "the gala carriages."

*Page 71*     THE COMTE DE CHAMBORD: the French prince Henri de Bourbon (1820–1883), duc de Bordeaux and comte de Chambord, who was unsuccessful in ascending the French throne after the death in exile of Charles X in 1836.

*Page 73*    "THE NIGHTDRESS IS TAKEN OFF . . . ": originally French, "la chemise est jetée pour l'amant, mais gardée pour le mari." Either a witticism or an unidentified French quotation.

*Page 74*    FREDERIK VI: king of Denmark in the years 1808 to 1839. To strengthen the weak and sickly boy, he was exposed to a treatment of cold baths and had to live without the usual royal luxuries.

*Page 75*    *EMMELINE:* presumably a mistaken reference to the novel by the English author Charlotte Smith, *Emmeline: The Orphan of the Castle* (1784). According to Pia Bondesson's catalogue of Blixen's books at her home, Rungstedlund, *Karen Blixen's bogsamling på Rungstedlund* (Copenhagen: Gyldendal/Karen Blixen Selskabet, 1982), KB owned *Nouvelles* (1841) by the French writer Alfred de Musset in a 1907 edition. One of the short stories from this collection, "Emmeline," might be another source of an erroneous quotation.

*Page 76*    "MAN AND WIFE WIPE . . .": not identified.

*Page 77*    JOHANNES EWALD, Danish poet and playwright, was one of Blixen's favorite writers. In 1773–76 he lived in the old Rungsted Inn, which eventually became the home of Karen Blixen and her family, Rungstedlund. There are many references to him in her work—see, e.g., "The Supper at Elsinore" from *Seven Gothic Tales*—and he is one of the main characters in "Converse at Night in Copenhagen" from *Last Tales*. When Karen Blixen died in 1962, she was buried at her own request on Ewald's Hill in the Rungstedlund park.

With his addiction to liquor, his dissipated lifestyle, and his tragic love affair with a girl who was made to marry another man, Ewald seems to have been a romantic figure to Blixen. This—and his beautiful ode "Rungsteds Lyksaligheder" ("The Delights of Rungsted," 1775)—seems to have been part of his attraction for her. The quotation is from "Sørgesange i Christinasborg Slots-Kirke den 18de Martius 1766 da Kong Frederick den Femte Skulde føres til sit Hvilested," elegies that Ewald wrote for the deceased King Frederik V (1766).

*Page 77*     KING FREDERIK V: the rather insignificant Danish king in the years 1746–66. He was rumored to have harbored sadistic tendencies and to have verged on insanity.

*Page 77*     THE *EDDA:* This name, which may be from the Icelandic *edda,* which means great-grandmother, or from Old Norse *odhr,* meaning poetry, is given to two works or collections, *The Elder* (or *Poetic*) *Edda,* and *The Younger* (or *Prose*) *Edda of Snorri Sturluson* (from the thirteenth century).

*Page 78*     RAGNAROK in the old Scandinavian mythology is the day of doom, when the world is to be destroyed to leave room for a new, peaceful world to come.

*Page 79*     "FEROCIOUS NECESSITY . . .": originally French, "la féroce nécessité, maîtresse des hommes et des dieux." The quotation has not been identified.

*Page 79*     FRANCIS I (1494–1547) was king of France in the years 1514–47. He was a full-blooded Renaissance prince who had many famous love affairs.

*Page 79*     "ALL THE LAWS . . .": originally French, "tous les lois du jeu divin" (i.e., love and lovemaking).

*Page 79*   A GRIM SHADOW: syphilis.

*Page 79*   "STUFF OF NATURE . . .": not identified.

*Page 79*   "A HARMONY BETWEEN DESIRE . . .": not identified.

*Page 81*   ZARATHUSTRA: from *Thus Spake Zarathustra* (1883–85), by Friedrich Nietzsche. The quotation is from the First Part, "On Little Old and Young Women."

*Page 82*   "HAD WEDDED WIVES . . .": not identified.

*Page 83*   A COURT AND SCHOOL OF LOVE: a judicial court for deciding matters of the heart, believed to have been established in Provence, France, and running from the eleventh to the fourteenth century. However, this "court of love" is now considered likely to be nothing but a literary device, not an actual institution.

*Page 84*   THE AESIR: a reference to "The Prophecy of the Seeress" from *The Poetic Edda,* which deals with life after Ragnarok (cf. notes to pages 77 and 78).

*Page 84*   PERCY BYSSHE SHELLEY. The quotation "in life's green grove" is from his lyrical drama *Prometheus Unbound* (1820), Act IV.

*Page 84*   THE DEMOGORGON was a terrible deity, first mentioned by the Christian writer Lactantius in the fifth century, who showed great courage since the very name of Demogorgon was considered lethal. In Shelley's *Prometheus Unbound,* this fearsome figure is the eternal principle that ousts false gods, thus imparting quite another quality to his character.

*Page 84*     KING LOUIS XVI (1754–1793) was the French king who was publicly executed by guillotine in Paris during the French Revolution, on January 21, 1793.

*Page 84*     14/7 1789 [July 14, 1789] was the crucial day in the French Revolution when the State prison, the Bastille, was seized by the mob. Judging by Louis XVI's diary, however, the significance of this event, which would eventually lead to his own death, seems to have escaped him entirely.

*Page 84*     PONTIUS PILATE, as the Roman governor of Judaea, was the one who had to pass sentence on Jesus, thus condemning him to death. During the Crucifixion, which of course was to change the outlook of the Western world, there was an earthquake that signified the exact moment of the death of Jesus (Matthew 27:52–54).

*Page 87*     CANAAN, the so-called Promised Land, was conquered by the Israelites in the thirteenth century.

*Page 88*     SAMUEL BUTLER, the English author and amateur biologist, developed his theory on evolution in four books beginning with *Life and Habit* (1878). The others were *Evolution, Old and New* (1879), *Unconscious Memory* (1880), and *Luck, or Cunning as the Main Means of Organic Modification?* (1887). In essence, he maintained that the many species did not develop, as Darwin claimed (cf. second note to page 32), through the agency of natural selection alone, but by means of the inheritable and purposeful exertions of individual organisms over countless generations. Consequently, all physical development was the result of an inherited but unconscious memory.

The quotation has not been verified, but the words

"zoosperm" for "spermatozoa" and "postnatal" for "prena-
tal" suggest that Blixen is not quoting Samuel Butler but
paraphrasing him, or perhaps quoting from memory.

Page 88   ANOTHER ENGLISH AUTHOR: the quotation has not been
verified and this author has not been identified.

Page 89   SHERLOCK HOLMES is the famous English detective in about
sixty stories by Sir Arthur Conan Doyle.

Page 90   MARTIN LUTHER (1483–1546), the German religious re-
former, who started the Protestant Reformation.

Page 91   MR. W. H.: William Shakespeare's still unidentified friend,
to whom his *Sonnets* (1609) were dedicated.

Page 91   "MAKE THEE ANOTHER SELF FOR LOVE OF ME": from Shakespeare's *Sonnets,* No. 10, "For shame! deny that thou bear'st
love to any. . . ."

Page 91   "NO LOVE TOWARDS OTHERS IN SUCH BOSOM SITS . . .": from
Shakespeare's *Sonnets,* No. 9, "Is it for fear to wet a
widow's eye. . . ."

Page 92   "THE MATERNAL INSTINCT . . .": from "Marriage" in the
"Maxims for Revolutionists," which forms part of the
notes to *Man and Superman* (1903) by George Bernard
Shaw.

Page 94   PAOLO was the brother-in-law of Francesca: these two Italian lovers were executed in 1289 for their adulterous affair.
Their story is told by various writers, most notably in the
poet Dante Alighieri's *Divina Commedia* (1302–21), in

which he depicts them as condemned souls—"Inferno," Canto V.

Page 94     NATHAN is the main character of the verse drama *Nathan the Wise* (1779) by Gotthold Ephraim Lessing. The plot turns on a discussion of the precedence of the three religions, Christianity, Islam, and Judaism. The Jew Nathan has to give his opinion, and his verdict is that they are of equal validity.

Page 94     URIAH THE HITTITE was married to the beautiful Bathsheba, with whom King David of Israel fell in love. When she became pregnant by the king, he put her husband to death by sending him to fight the enemy in the front line of the army (2 Samuel 11).

Page 94     KING SULEIMAN BEN DAOUD, i.e., King Solomon of Israel (died ca. 930 B.C.), was King David's son by Bathsheba. He was recognized as one of the wisest men of his age.

Page 94     CARDINAL JULES MAZARIN (1602–1661) was the Italian-born chief minister of France from 1642. He thus ruled the country during the minority of King Louis XIV (cf. second note to page 41).

Page 95     "MY WILL BE DONE, NOT THINE": a reverse paraphrase of Luke 22.42: "Father, if thou be willing, remove this cup from me; nevertheless, not my will, but thine, be done." (Jesus's prayer on Gethsemane before he was arrested and taken away to his subsequent conviction and Crucifixion.)

Page 95     HABR YUNIS was the tribe of Karen Blixen's trusted butler, Farah Aden (born ca. 1885, died during World War II), at the farm in Africa. In Chapter I, "The Ngong Farm," Part I, "Kamante and Lulu," in *Out of Africa,* she writes of the strong ties between the members of the tribe. When one of Farah's friends went to see somebody from a hostile tribe and met with an accident, it was seen as something he had deserved because of his "treason."

*Page 96*   PATRIOTS OF THE FORTIES is a reference to the European revolutions of 1948.

# Afterword: "On Modern Marriage" and the Twenties

## BY FRANK EGHOLM ANDERSEN

### Translated by Susan Petersen

Karen Blixen is often thought to have lived her life in dark and wild Africa until she was in her mid-forties. At that point, according to the myth, she returned to Europe to become a world-famous author, changing identity from one day to the next. Just like that: two separate lives that could only be connected backwards through art. Karen, the lioness of the bush, and Isak, the queen of the arts.

But this is far from the truth. She was a full-blooded European throughout her entire African life. More importantly, Karen Blixen was a European intellectual before Africa, in Africa, and when she returned again to Europe. During her entire life she was deeply engaged in the Western world's intellectual discussions and the spiritual currents of her times.

This could have been regarded as an undeniable fact. That Karen Blixen's identity as an intellectual is questioned at all is because she preferred to depict herself as the forsaken woman, forced to leave her property and lover in Africa and returning to Europe with neither hope nor future. Here it was of course necessary to earn a living, and, voilà, she then became an author.

She loved to live her life as theater. Nothing was allowed to remain what it immediately appeared to be: everything had to be a good show, to glow, throw off sparks, and first and foremost be part of a story she could produce or be co-producer of.

But her writing didn't actually fall from a clear blue sky. She wrote before Africa, in Africa, and out of Africa. And she wasn't so insignificant a philosopher; in any case she was a sharp critic of and shaper of her times. She was never merely a storyteller, as she preferred to call herself. It is precisely because of the deep roots she otherwise had in the times, its projects and concerns, that her later fairy tales could be told in a distant past, remaining totally outside the epoch, and outside history.

It is in this light that *On Modern Marriage and Other Observations* must be read, as an essay of and for its times. But what is it we are actually dealing with? The essay was originally written as a letter to her brother Thomas. Quite a long letter, one might say, and the "you" of the letter is not especially persistent, tending to fade out after the first paragraphs. The "you" is not intended for the brother, but for the epoch. The essay isn't a letter, but a philosophical contribution to the intellectual and cultural debate of the times—a contribution she didn't know where to send. Thomas, her favorite brother, had to take the place of the receiver.

Thomas was, however, not really an arbitrary second person with respect to the content of the essay, either. He was a member of the World League for Sexual Reform and participated in the organization's second world congress in Copenhagen in July 1928. The league was founded in 1927 by, among others, the Danish sexual reform activist Dr. J. H. Leunbach, and had as honorary presidents the Swiss August Forel and the Englishman

Havelock Ellis. Discussed at the congress were sexual reform, family planning, and sexual criminal law. In another letter to Thomas of October 10, 1926, Blixen writes:

> Now I believe that Denmark and Scandinavia, which take the lead in so many directions where progress is concerned, so that a man who is in the lead there will be in the forefront all over the world, in questions of sexual morality and birth control are officially surprisingly far behind. This is possibly because we are in fact so liberal that this whole problem has actually been solved without blows being struck, so that there has been no necessity for arguments and these are heard only as faint echos from without; possibly we are conservative about this,—I cannot judge of this since I am not conversant with "intellectual life" and conditions at home at all.[1]

In this letter we find a real "you." But we are dealing with another first person: a more modest and vague first person, who "cannot judge," "believes," and lets her sentences circle around the word "possibly." The first person of the essay is of another type, more poetic and visionary: "What fruits the trees bore here! All of those that human beings have seen in their most felicitous dreams: beauty, knowledge, eternal youth—indeed, everything you could wish for."

Darwin's *On the Origin of Species* appeared in 1859. Lamarck had already published his treatises *Philosophie zoologique, Histoire des animaux sans vertebras,* and *Systeme des connaissances positives* at the beginning of the century. In the course of the 1860s Sir Francis Galton introduced eugenics, a science devoted

---

[1] Isak Dinesen, *Letters from Africa 1914–1931* (London: Pan Books, 1983), p. 290.

to the improvement of the human race by careful selection of parents. From these beginnings in the second half of the nineteenth century, intellectuals from a variety of fields came to see as their task the creation of a theoretical basis on which it would be possible to define humanity in its ultimate utopian form.

One of the cornerstones of this theoretical project was the development of a selection procedure or test. How can a society determine who is sufficiently robust and suited to propagate themselves? How is one to judge who is not? Neo-Lamarckians and Darwinists discussed what test the giraffe had been through in the course of history in order to become worthy of bearing its long neck. The emergence of the young sciences criminology and sociology at the turn of the century can be related to a dream of developing an anatomical atlas capable of mapping out the correlation between physical characteristics and the soul's inner qualities and social abilities.

Another outgrowth of this debate and the endeavor to develop a test was an upswing in the development of big institutions such as asylums, prisons, mental hospitals, and institutions for the mentally retarded. At the heart of the interest in eugenics lay a utopian vision of the utmost human being in the utmost society. The means to that end would be the development of a battery of tests to define the human material that would create the basis for this construction. Who should be institutionalized, and who was robust, morally sound, and intelligent enough to remain outside? In 1865, Galton's model of social utopia was described in *Macmillan's Magazine* in the following way:

> His evidence justified him in putting forward a proposal or scheme, one of the most audacious ever formulated by a

sane man of science, that the State ought to select its most gifted young men and women in order to breed for genius. He even went so far as to write the speech which the "Senior Trustee of the Endowment Fund" was to address to the "ten deeply blushing young men of 25" who had issued successfully from the public examination which proved that they had "in the highest degree those qualities of body and mind which do most honour and service to our race."[2]

". . . who had issued successfully from the public examination." What kind of examination would be able to handle such a selection? For Galton, this wasn't a problem. Before the turn of the century hardly anyone questioned the absolute relationship between form (wealth, appearance, social status) and content (intelligence, talent, emotional stability). The general conviction was that anyone with an academic or inherited title could serve as a detective to track down inferior intelligence as well as immoral behavior and constitution. The justification for the test and the feasibility of its implementation were not questioned. Nature or God had created man in two separate classes, one of which was superior to the other. One aspect of this superiority consisted of the capacity to judge and evaluate the degree of the "lower" class's inferiority. The tremendous strength of conviction of those occupied with eugenics is clearly documented in a passage from Galton's book *Memories of My Life:* "Firstly, it [eugenics] must be made familiar as an academic question until its exact importance has been understood and accepted as a fact; secondly, it must be recognized as a subject whose practical

---

[2]Cited in Germaine Greer, *Sex and Destiny: The Politics of Human Fertility.* (London: Secker & Warburg, 1984), p. 259.

development deserves serious consideration into the national consciousness as a new religion."[3]

The problem of the test was not solved in the 1920s, but the interest in it remained. That is, in the technical side of it. How was one to segregate society's undesirable members and how could one possibly bring them to refrain from propagating themselves? Blixen's answer in *On Modern Marriage* is: let love decide. She draws marriage into the discussion—that institution that earlier had been considered the sole legitimate one for propagation—and reorganizes the discussion around the question of love. Love is the basis of the modern marriage, through which the race will be improved and the conditions of slavery and repression will be dissolved.

Karen Blixen's interest in *On Modern Marriage* has nothing at all to do with technical aspects, such as the battery of tests or how they could be developed. Rather, she is concerned with the actual essence of the selection procedure: what is man's most valuable quality, physical or intellectual equipment, wealth or social standing? None of these, according to Blixen's essay. It is the ability to love.

One of Blixen's intentions here was to reorganize the eugenics debate and its inherent contradictions so that it would be able to contribute to the discussion of the epoch's most existential problems. The twenties were the decade that still remembered the birth of the women's movement, the decade that experienced the explosion of interest in a variety of contraceptives and the marketing strategies that made them a part of the general knowledge of sexuality. The twenties were the decade that attempted to educate society so that the horrors of another world war could

---

[3]Ibid., p. 260.

be avoided. Furthermore, the twenties were that decade when women still remembered that they were capable of managing the general routines of society while the men were at war—and when women were not inclined to cast these experiences overboard without further ado. *On Modern Marriage* should be read as an effort to link the new "free" ideas of the twenties with the original potential of the theory of evolution.

But what were these new and free ideas that enlightened the twenties? In the previous century, the influence of genetic factors was used to explain social illnesses such as alcoholism, mental illness, criminality, mental retardation, birth defects, or simply the fact that one was born into a lower social class. Enlarging upon this theory, it was now believed that all such phenomena could be explained in terms of the interplay of various individual genes, first and foremost on the basis of experiments with fruit flies. These discoveries came to bear worldwide political consequences. For example, sterilization legislation was issued in several states in the United States. The attitude that led to the introduction of these laws could be epitomized by U.S. Supreme Court Justice Holmes's statement that "three generations of imbeciles are enough."[4]

Darwinism developed into Social Darwinism during the first decade of the century, in particular after the Mendelian laws of biology were applied to the study of evolution. The doctrine of degeneration resulting from this marriage was born in the awareness that humanity as a species was endangered by so-called undesirable elements, who propagated themselves at a faster rate than those regarded as valuable members of society. By linking

---

[4]Vogel and Motulsky, *History of Human Genetics* (New York: Springer Verlag, 1979), p. 14.

together inheritance and evolution, the important project became the isolation of "defective" individuals in order to prevent their damaging inheritance from being passed down to their offspring. It was a widespread conviction that this inheritance would continue to degenerate at an increasing rate over the course of several generations.

Eugenics and the doctrine of degeneration believed it possible to distinguish between morality and intelligence, and that by virtue of this distinction intelligence could be used for the purpose of categorization.

Denmark looked toward France, Italy, and the United States in these early days of categorization and intelligence-test development. In France, Alfred Binet and Théodore Simon, and in Italy, Sante de Sanctis, had developed batteries of tests that impressed Danish pioneers in the fields of special education and mental health. Christian Keller, one of the fathers of the Danish special education system, pleaded in 1912, "If only a few of the Scandinavian institutions also would run tests according to the Binet-Simon system."[5]

Keller was especially impressed by the Vineland Institution in New Jersey, which he described as a human laboratory where the scientific study of human development took place. Goddard, who was director of the institution, maintained that according to tests, two percent of Massachusetts schoolchildren were incapable of taking part in normal classroom instruction. He considered these children to be mentally deficient and abnormal, following the lines laid down by Binet. The tests could not have had the ideological and argumentative authority they held at the time if not for their claim that the results were constant for the tested

---

[5]*Nyt Tidskrift for Abnormvæsen,* 1910–12.

individual throughout his or her entire lifetime. Lewis Terman, the father of the American standardization of the Binet test, for example, asserted that on the basis of early test results he was able to predict later occupational placement.

Karen Blixen was all too modest when she wrote to Thomas: "I am not conversant with 'intellectual life' and conditions at home at all." She actually kept abreast of the European intellectual debate and took part in all sorts of conversations about conditions back home in Denmark. In the same letter to Thomas, she lets him know her opinion about the "war cries" of two of Denmark's most important participants in the epoch's sexual reform movement. She still considers herself capable of classifying the domestic Danish efforts as outdated and behind the times in comparison to the impressive international advances in the sexual reform movement: "But whatever the reason may be I am certain that the battle now being waged on the point at home is a thing of the past in the world at large, and that Thit Jensen's and Dr. Leunbach's war cries will not affect a single soul there."[6]

When it came to defining the relationship between the period's endeavor to categorize and the ideal model of humanity which she sensed lay behind the idea of selection, Blixen's formula was simple enough: fifty percent ability to love and fifty percent possibility for love. The essay begins with the Ideal and Nature and concludes with birth control and eugenics, but the conditions of love, socially and individually, are its driving force. The ideal for Blixen is what people desire to be or to become. If we wish hard enough to be able to fly to the moon, we will accomplish it—and she was right. If we desire to become every-

---

[6]*Letters from Africa*, p. 290.

thing for which we have the potential, then we can achieve it. Nature is nothing compared to the ideal—Blixen is in truth a Lamarckian, and one of the creative ones at that.

Her source of inspiration for the essay was first and foremost the Lamarckians, who rejected Darwin and everything he stood for with all their being. What he had come to stand for was embodied in his successors, whose "only idea of investigation was to imitate 'Nature' by perpetrating violent and senseless cruelties, and watch the effect of them with a paralyzing fatalism which forbade the smallest effort to use their minds instead of their knives and eyes. . . ."[7]

One of the period's most important neo-Lamarckians was George Bernard Shaw. He had a peculiar habit of writing long, philosophical prefaces to his plays, explaining how the ideas of the piece should fit into, or most often, not fit into, the spirit of the times. Karen Blixen was familiar with these prefaces and *On Modern Marriage* owes a great deal to them. This is especially true of Shaw's prefaces to three plays, *Getting Married, Back to Methuselah,* and *Heartbreak House.*

In a letter dated October 7, 1923, to her mother, Ingeborg Dinesen, she asks: "Will you ask him [Thomas] too if he has read Bernard Shaw, if not he must really do so. I have been reading such a lot by him recently with enormous enjoyment, especially two of his most recent books, *Heartbreak House* and *Back to Methuselah.* The prefaces to both of them are some of the most interesting things I have read."[8]

In the preface to *Back to Methuselah,* Shaw lambasts one of

---

[7]George Bernard Shaw, "Back to Methuselah: A Metabiological Pentateuch. Preface: The Infidel Half Century," *Collected Plays with Their Prefaces* (London: The Bodley Head, 1972), p. 306.

[8]*Letters from Africa,* p. 171.

the Darwinists, a certain Weismann, who had a scientific habit of cutting off the tails of mice in the hope that after a few generation tailless mice would be born. But unfortunately for Weismann this hope was in vain, and in Blixen's opening comments in *On Modern Marriage* she alludes to Shaw's advice to Weismann:

> First he should have procured a colony of mice highly susceptible to hypnotic suggestion. He should then have hypnotized them into an urgent conviction that the fate of the musque world depends on the disappearance of its tail, just as some ancient and forgotten experimenter seems to have convinced the cats of the Isle of Man. Having thus made the mice desire to lose their tails with a life-or-death intensity, he would very soon have seen a few mice born with little or no tail . . . and the miracle of the tailless mouse completely achieved.[9]

Shaw is serious here, even though his style is ironic, and for Blixen this was the very truth—mouse or man, tail or no tail, ideal is stronger than nature—change does not occur as a result of violence or technical sophistication, but by virtue of the human capacity to wish and endeavor. Blixen writes in the opening of her essay: "The rule is always the same: what you wish for, you shall have," and Shaw writes in "The Advent of the Neo-Lamarckians": "I call special attention to Lamarck, who . . . really held as his fundamental proposition that living organisms change because they want to. If you have no eyes, and want to see, and keep trying to see, you will finally get eyes."[10]

---

[9]Shaw, *Collected Plays.*
[10]Ibid.

Blixen's views bear a likeness to the "free-love" movement from America in the 1870s. This movement opposed marriage as a social institution and justified divorce with the logic of eugenics. In 1870, two of the "free-lovers," Tennessee Claflin and Victoria Woodhull, argued that the entire system of marriage was an "obstacle to the regeneration of the race."[11] As an extension of this fact, the free-lovers believed that children born out of wedlock usually were superior to other children, because they were "love-children."

In her essay, Blixen also gives expression to the desirability of "love-children," and her logic is in a sense also of eugenic character. But she is still not a "free-lover." Her philosophical project in the essay is to tie the problem of eugenics to the theory of evolution with the help of her own concept of free love, which also can exist within the bounds of marriage. Of course it is not found only within marriage, and Blixen is opposed to marriage as a social institution. She does not define her new modern marriage in opposition to the old traditional marriage, but claims that there no longer necessarily must be an opposition between marriage and free love because marriage can now be entered into, as well as dissolved, on the basis of love or lack of the same.

Her complaint—as is Shaw's—is that a mix-up of the concepts of marriage and morality has occurred: "The confusion of marriage with morality has done more to destroy the conscience of the human race than any other single error." For her modern marriage should not be built on moral assumptions, but on love. She would like to see marriage recognized as a love relationship,

---

[11] *Woodhull and Claflin's Weekly* 1, no. 20 (October 1, 1870), 10, cited in Linda Gordon, *Woman's Body, Woman's Right: A Social History of Birth Control in America* (New York: Grossman Publishers, 1976), p. 122.

and abolish its status as the place for procreation, woman's prison of security, and man's domain of rule.

Blixen is fundamentally a true romantic a hundred years after Romanticism. One could well call her a neo-romantic, though such a categorization does not serve to shed light on either the times or Blixen's writings. She herself came from and sought after an upper-class lifestyle and privilege, and was therefore necessarily a child of the upper class's traditional and conservative ideologies. Her argumentation in the essay uses discursive elements from virtually all of the nineteenth century's ideological movements—from Romanticism to the "free-love" movement, from the theory of evolution to Neo-Lamarckism, and from eugenics to the debate on contraceptives.

In spite of the fact that Blixen wants everything, in spite of her preference for the mystical, which we see unfolding in her later tales, she is remarkably clearheaded in this essay. She in fact manages to tie together the structural content of the ideological debates, incorporating them into her concept of modern marriage and of the possible relationships between men and women.

It is important that *On Modern Marriage* is finally available in the English-speaking world, important to experience the twenties seen through the eyes of an international intellectual, important also in order to know the Karen Blixen who participated in the debates of her times. The essay is significant for the understanding of the rest of Isak Dinesen's writings. This is also important for a better understanding of ourselves, in which we see revealed a combination of the element of love and the element of ambition or desire.

# SELECTED BIBLIOGRAPHY

## Karen Blixen's Writings in English

Except for a few pieces, Karen Blixen until 1963 wrote everything in English first and then translated it into Danish. *Carnival: Entertainments and Posthumous Tales* is partly in her own English, partly in translation. The letters were translated by Anne Born.

*Seven Gothic Tales.* New York: Harrison Smith & Robert Haas, 1934; London: Putnam, 1934 (Denmark in 1935).

*Out of Africa.* London: Putnam, 1937; New York: Random House, 1938.

*Winter's Tales.* New York: Random House, 1942; London: Putnam: 1942.

*The Angelic Avengers* (pseudonym: Pierre Andrezel). London: Putnam, 1946; New York: Random House, 1947 (Denmark in 1944).

*Last Tales.* London: Putnam, 1957; New York: Random House, 1957.

*Anecdotes of Destiny.* London: Michael Joseph, 1958; New York: Random House, 1958.

*Shadows on the Grass.* London: Michael Joseph, 1960; New York: Random House, 1961.

*Ehrengard.* London: Michael Joseph, 1963; New York: Random House, 1963.

*The Revenge of Truth.* In Donald Hannah, *Isak Dinesen and Karen Blixen: The Mask and the Reality.* London: Putnam, 1971 (Denmark in 1926, *Tilskueren,* May).

*Carnival: Entertainments and Posthumous Tales.* Chicago: University of Chicago Press, 1979 (Denmark in 1975).

*Daguerreotypes and Other Essays,* translated by P. M. Mitchell and W. D. Paden. Chicago: University of Chicago Press, 1979.

*Letters from Africa 1914–1931,* edited by Frans Lasson and translated by Anne Born. Chicago: University of Chicago Press, 1981 (Denmark in 1981).

*BLIXENIANA 1983: Karen Blixen's Juvenilia. A Critical Selection,* by Else Cederborg. Copenhagen: Gyldendal/Karen Blixen Selskabet, 1983 (in Danish only). (*BLIXENIANA* was the yearbook of the now dissolved Karen Blixen Society, edited by Hans Andersen and Frans Lasson.)

# Biographies

Bjørnvig, Thorkild. *The Pact: My Friendship with Isak Dinesen.* Baton Rouge, La.: Louisiana State University Press, 1983.

Dinesen, Thomas. *Tanne. Min søster Karen Blixen (Tanne: My Sister Karen Blixen).* Copenhagen: Gyldendal, 1974 (in Danish only).

Lasson, Frans, and Svendsen, Clara, eds. *The Life and Destiny of Isak Dinesen.* Chicago and London: Phoenix Edition, University of Chicago Press, 1976.

Migel, Parmenia. *Titania: The Biography of Isak Dinesen.* New York: Random House, 1967.

Svendsen, Clara, ed. *Isak Dinesen: A Memorial.* New York: Random House, 1965.

*Notater om Karen Blixen (Notes on Karen Blixen).* Copenhagen: Gyldendal, 1974 (in Danish only).

Thurman, Judith. *Isak Dinesen: The Life of a Storyteller.* New York: St. Martin's Press, 1982.

Trzebinski, Errol. *Silence Will Speak: A Study of the Life of Denys Finch Hatton and His Relationship with Karen Blixen.* London: William Heinemann, 1977.

## Books on Kenya, Colonialism, and White Settlers

Fox, James. *White Mischief.* London: Jonathan Cape, 1982.

Huxley, Elspeth. *The Flame Trees of Thika: Memories of an African Childhood.* London: Chatto & Windus, 1959.

———. *The Mottled Lizard.* London: Chatto & Windus, 1962.

———. *White Man's Country: Lord Delamere and the Making of Kenya.* London: Chatto & Windus, 1968.

———, and Curtis, Arnold, eds. *Pioneer's Scrapbook: Reminiscences of Kenya, 1890 to 1968.* London: Evans Brothers, 1980.

JanMohamed, Abdul R. *Manichean Aesthetics: The Politics of Literature in Colonial Africa.* Amherst, Mass.: University of Massachusetts Press, 1983.

———. "The Economy of Manichean Allegory: The Function of Racial Difference in Colonialist Literature." *Critical Inquiry,* vol. 12, no. 1 (Autumn 1985).

Leakey, Louis Seymour. *Kenya: Contrasts and Problems.* Cambridge, Mass.: Schenkman, 1966 (1st edn. 1935).

Low, Donald Anthony, and Smith, Alison, eds. *The History of East Africa.* Oxford: The Clarendon Press, 1976.

Seaton, Henry. *Lion in the Morning.* London: John Murray, 1963.

## Books and Articles on Karen Blixen's Writings

Aikcn, Susan Hardy. "Dinesen's 'Sorrow-Acre': Tracing the Woman's Line." *Contemporary Literature,* vol. 25, 1984.

Bondesson, Pia. *Karen Blixen's bogsamling på Rungstedlund: En katalog (Karen Blixen's Book Collection at Rungstedlund: A Catalogue,* in Danish only). Copenhagen: Gyldendal/Karen Blixen Selskabet, 1982.

Brøgger, Suzanne. *Deliver Us from Love* (essay collection with one essay on Karen Blixen). New York: Delacorte Press, 1976.

Burstein, Janet Handler. "Two Locked Caskets: Selfhood and 'Otherness' in the Work of Isak Dinesen." *Texas Studies in Literature and Language,* vol. 20, 1978.

Cederborg, Else. "Den camouflereded modstand: Karen Blixens kvindesyn" ("Camouflaged Resistance: Karen Blixen's View of Women," in Danish only). *Edda,* no. 1, 1979.

———: *"Det drømmende Barn" og andre fortaellinger af Karen Blixen ("The Dreaming Child" and Other Tales by Karen Blixen,* in Danish only). Copenhagen: Dansklaerererforeningen/Gyldendal, 1979.

———: *BLIXENIANA 1983* (a critical selection of Karen Blixen's juvenilia, in Danish only). Copenhagen: Gyldendal Karen Blixen Selskabet, 1983.

———: "Mytologien som forløsningsmodel i Karen Blixens 'Karyatiderne, en ufuldendt Historie,' 1938/1957" ("Mythology as a Model of Redemption in Karen Blixen's 'The Caryatids, an Unfinished Tale,' 1938–57, in Danish only). *Edda,* no. 1, 1984.

Gubar, Susan. " 'The Blank Page' and the Issues of Female Creativity." *Critical Inquiry,* no. 8 (Winter 1981). (Reprinted in Elaine Showalter, ed., *Feminist Criticism. Essays on Women, Literature and Theory.* New York: Pantheon Books, Random House, 1985.)

Hannah, Donald. *"Isak Dinesen" and Karen Blixen: The Mask and the Reality.* London: Putnam, 1971.

Henriksen, Liselotte. *Karen Blixen: En bibliografi/Isak Dinesen: A Bibliography* (partly in Danish, partly in English). Copenhagen: Gyldendal, 1977.

James, Sibyl. "Gothic Transformations: Isak Dinesen and the Gothic." In J. E. Fleenor, ed., *The Female Gothic.* London: Eden, 1983.

Johannesson, Eric O. *The World of Isak Dinesen.* Seattle: The University of Washington Press, 1961.

Juhl, Marianne, and Jørgensen, Bo Hakon. *Diana's Revenge: Two Lines in Isak Dinesen's Authorship* (translated from the Danish by Anne Born). Odense, Denmark: Odense University Press, 1985 (address: 36 Pjentedamsgade, Odense, DK-5000 C, Denmark).

Langbaum, Robert. *The Gayety of Vision: A Study of Isak Dinesen's Art.* London: Chatto & Windus, 1964.

Lewis, Florence C. "Isak Dinesen and Feminist Criticism." *The North American Review* (Spring 1979).

Lydenberg, Robin. "Against the Law of Gravity: Female Adolescence in Isak Dinesen's *Seven Gothic Tales.*" *Modern Fiction Studies,* vol. 24 (1978–79).

Scholtz, Nini Marquart. "From Revenge to Reconciliation: Truth as a Theme in the Work of Isak Dinesen." *Scandinavica,* vol. 12, 1973.

Schow, H. Wayne. "Karen Blixen and Martin A. Hansen: Art, Ethics, and the Human Condition." *Scandinavian Studies,* vol. 52, 1980.

Stambaugh, Sara. "Imagery of Entrapment in the Fiction of Isak Dinesen." *Scandinavica,* vol. 22, 1983.

Stephens, Anthony. "The Paradox of the Omnipotent Narrator in the Work of Karen Blixen." *Neophilologus,* vol. 62, 1978.

Weed, Merry. "Märchen and Legend Tradition of Narrative in Two 'Tales' of Isak Dinesen." *Journal of Folklore Institute* (Bloomington, Ind.), vol. 15, 1978.

Whissen, Thomas R. *Isak Dinesen's Aesthetics.* New York: Kennikat Press, 1973.

——. "The Bow of the Lord: Isak Dinesen's Portrait of the Artist." *Scandinavian Studies,* vol. 46, 1974.

## *Miscellaneous*

de Beauvoir, Simone. *The Second Sex,* translated and edited by H. M. Parshley. New York: Alfred A. Knopf, 1953.

Figes, Eva. *Sex & Subterfuge: Women Writers to 1850.* London: Macmillan, 1982.

Fleenor, Julian E., ed. *The Female Gothic.* London: Eden, 1983.

Marks, Elaine, and de Courtivron, Isabelle, eds. *New French Feminisms: An Anthology.* Amherst, Mass.: University of Massachusetts Press, 1980.

Moers, Ellen. *Literary Women.* New York: Anchor Books, Anchor Press/Doubleday, 1977.

Showalter, Elaine. *A Literature of Their Own: British Women Novelists from Brontë to Lessing.* London: Virago Press, 1977.

———, ed. *Feminist Criticism: Essays on Women, Literature, and Theory.* New York: Pantheon Books, Random House, 1985.

Spacks, Patricia Meyer. *The Female Imagination.* New York: Avon Books, 1972.